DISCOVERING LANGUAGES
FRENCH

TEACHER'S EDITION

Elaine S. Robbins

Formerly Mount Logan Middle School
Logan, Utah

Kathryn R. Ashworth

Brigham Young University

AMSCO SCHOOL PUBLICATIONS, INC.
315 Hudson Street / New York, N.Y. 10013

Cassettes

The DISCOVERING LANGUAGES series includes two cassettes for each language, except Latin. The voices are those of native speakers.

Each cassette includes the following material:

Oral exercises in four-phased sequences: cue—pause for student response—correct response by native speaker—pause for student repetition.

The dialogs at normal listening speed.

Questions or completions in four-phased sequences.

Seven or eight songs for each language, sung with accompaniment.

The French cassettes (Ordering Code N 591 C) are available separately from the publisher. A complete cassette script is included.

When ordering this book, please specify R 591 T or
DISCOVERING LANGUAGES: FRENCH, TEACHER'S EDITION

ISBN 1-56765-304-9

Printed in the United States of America

4 5 6 7 8 9 10   02 01 00

Preface

DISCOVERING LANGUAGES is a four-color foreign language program consisting of five separate texts: French, German, Italian, Spanish, and Latin. An additional component, *Origins and History of Language,* suitable for reproduction, is an integral part of the program and is included in this Teacher's Edition. DISCOVERING LANGUAGES is designed for either a one-year or one-semester course in upper-elementary or middle-school Foreign Language Exploratory programs, commonly known as FLEX. The DISCOVERING LANGUAGES Program aims to:

➡ Offer students an opportunity to begin communicating in different foreign languages in a formal course before choosing one language for further study.

➡ Foster a global perspective by exposing students to several foreign languages, the countries where they are spoken, and the people who speak them.

➡ Heighten students' appreciation and respect for cultural diversity and sharpen their cross-cultural awareness and sensitivity.

➡ Introduce students to the rich ethnic heritage of the English language and provide them with an insight into the nature of language, its origins and early development, language families, and similarities among languages.

➡ Develop interdisciplinary skills by linking foreign language study with language arts, social studies, and math.

DISCOVERING LANGUAGES is designed to give students the opportunity to begin communicating in a foreign language in a natural, personalized, enjoyable, and rewarding context. Communication is developed through simple materials in visually focused topical contexts.

The text for each language of the DISCOVERING LANGUAGES Program includes an introduction to the specific country, its language and people. A final review section practices and reinforces the vocabulary and culture taught in preceding sections. Illustrated cultural notes offer views and insights into aspects of foreign life that students can easily relate to their own lives.

Each section includes a variety of activities designed to give students the feeling that not only can they learn all that has been presented but that they can also have fun practicing the foreign language. Activities include dialogs in cartoon-strip fashion, picture-cued exercises and puzzles, skits and conversa-

activities, songs, and games. The words and expressions as well as the language structures introduced in DISCOVERING LANGUAGES have been carefully chosen and limited to insure student comfort and success.

Origins and History of Language

A sixteen-page discussion of origins and history of language, suitable for reproduction, is included in each Teacher's Edition. It covers prehistoric messages, early systems of writing, early alphabets, languages of Europe, history of the English language, the Latin-English connection, and language richness of American place names. An integral component of DISCOVERING LANGUAGES, this unit provides an interesting introduction to the program.

Vocabulary

Each section begins with topically related illustrations that convey the meanings of new words in the target language without recourse to English. This device enables students to make a direct and vivid association between the foreign terms and their meanings. Most activities use illustrations and picture cues to practice words and expressions.

To facilitate comprehension, an early section of each book is devoted to cognates of English words. Beginning a course in this way shows students that the target language is not so "foreign" after all and helps them overcome any fears they may have about the difficulty of learning a language. Words and expressions are limited and structure is simple and straightforward. Because students are not overburdened, they quickly gain a feeling of success.

Conversation

Students learn to express themselves and talk about their families and friends. They learn to greet people, to tell the day and month of the year, to identify and describe people and objects, and more. Skits and conversational activities follow situational dialogs in cartoon-strip style, encouraging students to begin using the target language for communication and self-expression. These activities serve as a springboard for personalized communication in pairs or groups.

Pronunciation

Throughout each book of the series, a lively and often humorous cartoon-strip detective character will guide students on how to pronounce the sounds and words of the particular language.

Songs

Each language component, except Latin, includes seven or eight songs in its Teacher's Edition, incorporating much of the vocabulary of the book and providing an amusing and effective learning tool. The songs include numbers, days of the week, colors, parts of the body, and more. Musical arrangements and lyrics, as well as English translations, are provided in the Teacher's Editions and the cassette scripts.

Culture

The first section of each book introduces students to the foreign language, its speakers, and the countries where it is spoken. Illustrated cultural notes follow most sections and offer students a variety of views and insights into well-known and not so well-known aspects of the culture: school, holidays, leisure time, sports, and interesting manners and customs.

Teacher's Editions

The Teacher's Edition for each language provides a wealth of suggestions and strategies for teaching all elements in the book. Also included are supplementary listening and speaking activities, total physical response activities, projects and research topics, and additional cultural information to supplement the cultural notes in the student book. The Teacher's Editions also include musical arrangements and lyrics for the target language songs together with English translations for the songs and a complete Key to all exercises and puzzles.

Cassettes

Two cassettes with a printed script are available from the publisher for each language except Latin. They include oral exercises, questions, completions, and dialogs, all with appropriate pauses for response or repetition. The cassettes also include the songs in the Teacher's Editions, sung with accompaniment.

Teacher Preparation

The DISCOVERING LANGUAGES Program is designed with the foreign-language teacher as well as the non-foreign-language teacher in mind. The simple and straightforward vocabulary and structures taught in the course can be easily mastered by teachers with little knowledge of the target language. Instructors with no knowledge of the foreign language will find the Teacher's Edition and the cassette accompanying each language component particularly useful tools.

Origins and History of Language

1 Prehistoric Messages

About one hundred years ago, river pebbles were discovered under layers of debris in a cave in southern France. These pebbles, untouched for tens of thousands of years, were decorated with lines and dots of a red paint called ocher. The markings resembled a form of writing. What was the purpose of these marked pebbles? Scientists guessed that they were good-luck charms, but no one knew with certainty.

In the early 1960s, the scientist Alexander Marshack discovered prehistoric bones gouged with scratches and marks. He explained these markings as examples of early people's efforts to count, tally, and number objects. Many similar bones have been found since that time.

As early as thirty thousand years ago, cave dwellers in Spain and France told stories about hunting by painting pictures on cave walls. These picture stories are the earliest known examples of "written" ideas. A cave in Altamira, Spain, contains some of the most important examples of cave art. The pictures at Altamira show bisons, wild horses, deer with huge antlers, and strange prehistoric creatures in yellow, red, brown, and black. What inspired these pictures? What was their purpose? Some have guessed that primitive people painted these scenes to bring them luck in the hunt.

For thousands of years, people expressed themselves by drawing, painting, and etching on rocks and other surfaces. Storytelling pictures in caves have been discovered in many areas of the world. From them we have learned much about how prehistoric people built huts, plowed, planted, and performed a variety of other activities. They give us a glimpse into the life and customs of prehistoric people.

Stone markings, cave paintings, and bone decorations are the earliest forms of "written" communication. Although spoken language came before written language, we do not know how prehistoric people spoke. Did they communicate by making animal sounds? For example, did they refer to a cat by making the sound *meow*, and did *meow* then become the word for cat? These and many other questions may never be answered.

Activity A

1. Where and when were pebbles with primitive markings resembling writing discovered?

_____

2. What did the markings mean?

_____

3. Which came first, speaking or writing?

_____

4. How many years ago were animals painted in the cave in Altamira, Spain?

_____

5. What can we learn from cave art?

_____

2 Early Systems of Writing

Over many thousands of years, people invented and discovered ways to improve their lives. They learned to raise crops by using irrigation; they learned to weave cloth, to build houses, chariots, ships with sails; and they developed tools and weapons. They began to live in cities and trade the goods they produced. As life grew more and more complex, it became essential to find a way to record and communicate the ever-increasing amount of information people had to remember. And so people began to write.

The earliest people to develop a form of writing were the Sumerians, who lived in an ancient land called Mesopotamia, known today as Iraq, about five thousand years ago.

The Sumerians advanced far beyond their neighbors because their efficient method of writing replaced complicated pictures or scratches on bones. At first the Sumerians created a system of writing made up of many simplified pictures that stood for words. For example, a crown would mean king, a spear would mean kill, waves would mean sea, and so on. The next step the Sumerians took to make their writing less complicated is the single most important step in the history of writing. To make it easier to understand this important step, let's pretend that the Sumerians spoke English.

At the beginning, Sumerians used one picture for every word in their language. To write the word *sea*—the body of water—they used one picture, ~~~, and to write the verb *to see* they used another picture, 👁 👁 . At a certain point, the Sumerians realized that two different pictures were not necessary to express the same-sounding word. So they began to use one picture for both words. For example, they chose this picture, ~~~ , to write both the words *sea* and *to see*.

With time, they went one step further. They began to use the picture ~~~ whenever the sound *see* occurred WITHIN a word. For the word *season,* for example, they used the symbol ~~~ followed by the symbol for *sun* and wrote *season* like this: ~~~ + ○ .

If we wrote English using the Sumerian way of writing, this is how we would write the following words:

kitten

starfish

And these sentences would be written as follows:

Aunt saw king.

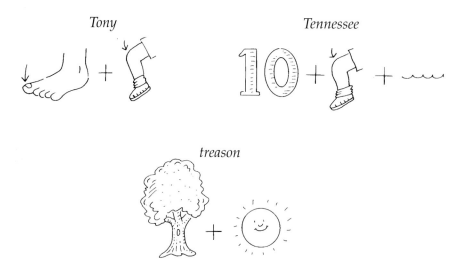

King told seaman to sail.

Having picture symbols stand for sounds not only cut down on the thousands of pictures the Sumerians needed to remember but also made it possible to write words that could not be illustrated with a picture, such as names of people, cities, and abstract words. Here are some examples:

Tony   *Tennessee*

treason

Does this remind you of a game? You have probably played the rebus game. That is exactly how writing began.

Activity B

Now you try. Write the following words using the rebus principle:

1. penmanship _____

2. horseshoe   _____

3. many   _____

4. penny   _____

5. seesaw   _____

6. skinny   _____

7. heartless   _____

8. heartburn   _____

9. tighten   _____

10. timeless   _____

11. cowboy   _____

12. kitten   _____

3 Early Alphabets

In order to write in ancient Sumerian, hundreds of symbols had to be memorized and the symbols had to be carefully written. Since it was difficult for everyone to learn so many symbols, writing became the job of a small number of people called scribes. In time, scribes improved and simplified the symbols of the written language in order to make their work easier.

It took the Sumerians a long time to come up with an efficient and accurate writing system known as cuneiform. The Sumerians pressed their writing instruments into clay tablets while the clay was damp and soft. Some of their neighbors—the Babylonians, the Assyrians, and the Persians—borrowed the idea of writing from the Sumerians and adapted it to the sounds of their own languages.

The ancient Egyptians developed a different writing system. Like the Sumerians, they also used symbols and signs that stood for words and parts of words, but they created symbols called hieroglyphs. They wrote on papyrus scrolls instead of clay tablets. Papyrus was a paperlike material made from the fibers of reeds that grew along the Nile River.

The next important step in the history of writing was taken by the Phoenicians, who lived along the easternmost coast of the Mediterranean Sea. They realized the value of writing but found the picture writing of the Egyptians complicated and awkward. Instead, the Phoenicians developed a system of only 22 to 30 symbols. This system was not like the Sumerian and Egyptian writing systems where a picture symbol stood for a whole word or part of a word. In the Phoenician writing system, one symbol stood for a single consonant plus a vowel sound.

The alphabet was the next step. When the Greeks started using separate symbols for vowels and consonants, the first true alphabet was created.

The alphabet developed by the Greeks was to become the foundation of the Roman alphabet, which is very similar to the one we use today. The Greeks also gave us the word *alphabet*. *Alpha* is the first letter of the Greek alphabet, and *beta* is the second.

Now compare the different writing systems illustrated on page *xiii*. Note that the Egyptian symbols date back to 3000 B.C., the Phoenician symbols to 1000 B.C., the Greek alphabet to 600 B.C., and the Roman alphabet to A.D. 114. Capital letters were the only forms used in the Greek and Roman alphabets. Lower-case letters developed gradually from the small letters used by scribes who needed to fit more words in the books they copied by hand.

The Roman alphabet closely resembles our modern alphabet except for the letters *J, U,* and *W,* which were added to the alphabet during the Middle Ages.

Egyptian	Phoenician	Greek	Roman
		A	A
		B	B
		Γ	C
		Δ	D
		E	E
		F	F
		Γ	G
		A	H
		I	I
		I	I
		K	K
		Λ	L
		M	M

Egyptian	Phoenician	Greek	Roman
		N	N
		O	O
		Γ	P
		Q	Q
		P	R
		Σ	S
		T	T
		Υ	V
		Υ	V
		Υ	V
		X	X
		Υ	Y
		Z	Z

Activity C

1. Who were the people who made cuneiform writings on clay tablets?

_____

2. What was the name of the land where these people lived?

_____

3. Why did the Sumerians need to invent writing?

_____

4. Did every Sumerian learn cuneiform writing? Why or why not?

_____

5. What was the writing of the ancient Egyptians called?

_____

6. How was Phoenician writing different from hieroglyphics and cuneiform writing?

_____

7. What was the name of the people who invented the true alphabet?

_____

8. Where does the word *alphabet* come from?

_____

4 The Languages of Europe

About three thousand languages are spoken around the world. All these languages have been grouped into nine major families. Language families are groups of languages that are related because they developed from a single common language called the parent language.

Indo-European is the most widespread language family in the world. About half of the world's population today speaks an Indo-European language, including most of the people of modern Europe. All the Indo-European languages came from the same parent language. Although there are no records of the parent language, scientists believe that a very long time ago speakers of this language lived in central Europe. As these people grew in number, they moved into other areas of the European continent and of the world. Some went to the country we now call Greece. Others went to Italy, France, and England. Some moved north to the Baltic countries, and still others went east to Russia. The farthest any of these people are believed to have gone is Asia Minor and northern India.

These groups took their language with them, but once they were separated from one another, the parent language they all spoke began to change. Now, after thousands of years, the language of each group has changed so much that one group cannot understand the other.

The Indo-European family of languages is divided into several smaller groups or subgroups. The following is a partial list of these subgroups and the modern languages that evolved from them:

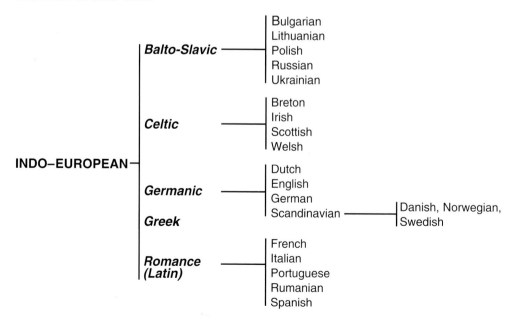

Activity D

Now with your teacher's help, look at a world map and identify those countries whose languages belong to the Indo-European family of languages.

Although the sounds and forms of the original Indo-European parent language have changed, many of its basic words are still found in different modern languages today.

Look at the similarities in these examples:

ENGLISH	LATIN	ITALIAN	FRENCH	SPANISH	GERMAN
circus	circus	circo	cirque	circo	Zirkus
mother	mater	madre	mère	madre	Mutter
nature	natura	natura	nature	naturaleza	Natur
nose	nasus	naso	nez	nariz	Nase
stadium	stadium	stadio	stade	estadio	Stadion

English derived from the Germanic subgroup, but it also contains many words of the Romance subgroup of languages.

The three most widely spoken languages of the Western Hemisphere are English, Spanish, and Portuguese. French, another European language, is also spoken by several million people in eastern Canada and the Caribbean. English, Spanish, Portuguese, and French explorers and settlers were the first Europeans to bring their languages to the New World.

Languages are always changing. As we speak, new words are being created and added to our own English language. Every new discovery in science and technology, for example, requires a new word. Think about it. Did the words *laser* and *compact disc* exist fifty years ago?

New words are also added to English when words are borrowed from other languages. In English, for example, we use the German words **gesundheit** and **pumpernickel,** the French words **ballet** and **boutique,** the Italian words **maestro** and **fiasco,** and the Spanish words **pimiento** and **patio.**

Activity E

1. Name the three leading languages of the Western Hemisphere.

_____

2. Name a fourth European language, which is spoken in eastern Canada.

_____

3. What is the name of the language family from which scientists think most European languages came?

_____

4. Name five modern languages of the Romance language subgroup.

_____

5. English is a combination of which two language subgroups?

_____

6. Name five words that have been created and added to English in the last fifty years.

_____

7. Name five foreign words that English has borrowed from other languages.

_____

5 History of the English Language

English is the most widely spoken language in the world today. The origins of the English language go way back to a language spoken more than two thousand years ago by people called the Celts, who lived in what is now England.

The history of the English language can be divided into three periods:

1. The Old English period, from 500 to 1000
2. The Middle English period, from 1100 to 1500
3. The Modern English period, from 1500 to the present

During this long span of time, England was invaded and ruled by people from different areas of Europe, each bringing with them their own languages.

First came the Romans who conquered England and ruled over the Celts from 50 B.C. to A.D. 400. Around A.D. 450, three Germanic tribes known as the Jutes, the Angles, and the Saxons invaded England. These tribes brought with them Germanic languages that resemble modern German. With time these languages mixed to form what is called Old English, also known as Anglo-Saxon.

During the mid-1000s, the Normans, a people living in northern France, invaded England. They brought with them the French language of the time. The people of England borrowed thousands of French words and made them part of their own language. The pronunciation and word order of Old English also changed under the influence of the Normans.

In addition to French, a great number of Latin words entered the language spoken in England. Latin was an influential language used by church officials and courts of law. The language that resulted from the mixture of Old English, French, and Latin is called Middle English.

By the sixteenth century, Middle English had changed so much that a person who spoke Old English would not have understood it. Over the next few hundred years, English borrowed words from many different languages and slowly developed into Modern English.

Beginning in the 1600s, the English language began to spread across the world as the English explored and colonized North America, Africa, Australia, and India.

6 The Latin-English Connection

More than half of all English words come from Latin. Some English words are spelled exactly like Latin: **odor, color, circus.** In many other words, the only difference between English and Latin is one or two letters: **machina, natura, familia.**

Here is a list of Latin words and their meanings. Now look at the English word that came from the Latin word. Write the definition of each of the English words in the empty boxes.

LATIN	MEANING	ENGLISH	DEFINITION
agricola	*farmer*	agriculture	
canis	*dog*	canine	
digitus	*finger*	digit	
femina	*woman*	feminine	
lavare	*to wash*	lavatory	
salutare	*to greet*	salute	
venditare	*to sell*	vendor	
laborare	*to work*	laboratory	

Now look at these Latin words and their meanings. Find an English word that comes from the Latin. You may be able to come up with more than one English word. An example is given to get you started.

LATIN	MEANING	ENGLISH WORD(S)
pedis	*foot*	pedal, pedicure, pedestrian
aqua	*water*	
dentis	*teeth*	
libri	*books*	
frigidus	*cold*	
vocabulum	*word*	
spectare	*to watch*	
portare	*to carry*	
lavare	*to wash*	
computare	*to count, do figures*	

Many other English words are often made up of two Latin words. For example, the English word *submarine* comes from the Latin prefix **sub-** meaning "under" and the Latin root (or base) **marinus** meaning "sea." The short Latin word **sub-** is called a prefix because it is placed before the root. Look at how it works:

PREFIX	+	ROOT	=	LITERAL ENGLISH MEANING	ENGLISH WORD
sub-	+	**marinus**	=	*under the sea*	*submarine*

Now you do it. Here is a list of common prefixes + root words and their meanings. Can you combine them to form English words ? Write the literal English meaning and the English word in the empty boxes. Some examples are given to get you started.

PREFIX	+	ROOT	=	LITERAL ENGLISH MEANING	ENGLISH WORD
in- *in, into*	+	**vadere** *to advance*	=	*to advance into*	*invade*
circum- *around*	+	**navigare** *to sail*	=	*to sail around*	*circumnavigate*
ex- *out of, from*	+	**portare** *to carry*	=		
im- *in, into*	+	**portare** *to carry*	=		
trans- *across*	+	**portare** *to carry*	=		
in- *in, into*	+	**habitare** *to live*	=		
intro- *in, inward*	+	**ducere** *to lead*	=		
inter- *between*	+	**rumpere** *to break*	=		
sub- *under*	+	**terrenus** *earth*	=		
suc- *up*	+	**cedere** *to go*	=		
pro *forward*	+	**cedere** *to go*	=		

As you can see, the Latin-English connection is a strong one. If we took a closer look at German, as well as other European languages, we would also find thousands of words that resemble English. By learning a foreign language not only are we able to communicate with and appreciate people from different countries and cultures, we also learn a lot about our own language, English.

7 Language Richness of American Place Names

Spanish Place Names

The Spanish language first came to America in 1492 with Christopher Columbus's expedition. In the following years, Spanish spread across the lands conquered and settled by Spanish explorers.

Many names of American cities, especially in the West, come from Spanish. Las Vegas (Nevada) means "the meadows"; Sacramento (California) means "sacrament"; Pueblo (Colorado) means "town"; and Los Angeles (California) means "the angels." San Francisco is Spanish for "Saint Francis," and San Diego for "Saint James."

There are Spanish place names for states as well. Florida was originally called **Pascua Florida,** Spanish for "flowered Easter." Montana means "mountain." Colorado comes from the Spanish word **colorado** meaning "colored" or "reddish," the color of the Colorado River when it carries a load of silt through the red rock country it crosses.

Many other Spanish place names are found in the East, West, and Southwest. The mountain range between Nevada and California is called the Sierra Nevada, Spanish for "snowy mountain range." The Alamo in Texas is Spanish for "poplar tree," a tree that grew where settlers found water.

Native American Place Names

Native Americans lived in North America before the Spanish, English, or French settled in America. The Mohawks, Oneidas, Onondagas, Cayugas, and Senecas made up the five Iroquois nations of central New York. Many American Indian words remain for states, cities, mountains, and rivers in that area and across the United States. Lakes Michigan, Huron, and Erie, as well as the Mississippi and Missouri rivers, come from Indian names. These names were also given to cities and states. Other state names that came from the Indians are Illinois, Massachusetts, Minnesota, Alaska, Connecticut, and Utah.

English Place Names

The East Coast of the United States was colonized by the English, and many of its place names are of English origin. The Puritans who sailed on the *Mayflower* named Plymouth after an English city. The cities of Boston, Bristol, Cambridge, Kent, and Lancaster were named after towns and counties in England.

The English also named cities in honor of their kings, queens, and nobility. Jamestown, Virginia, an early colony, is named after King James I. New York is named in honor of the Duke of York, brother of King Charles II.

The names of English explorers are also found on the map of the United States. Henry Hudson sailed up the East Coast and into the river later named in his honor. Pennsylvania honors its founder, the Quaker leader William Penn. Baltimore, Maryland, is named after its founder, Lord Baltimore.

French Place Names

French explorers and settlers also named places after French cities, kings, and explorers. New Orleans is named after the French city of **Orléans** saved by the heroic Joan of Arc, who led the French army against an English invasion. Louisiana was named for King Louis XIV, the king of France when the territory of Louisiana was explored and claimed by French explorers.

Provo, Utah, was named after Étienne Provost, a French-Canadian fur trader. Des Moines, Iowa, means "of the monks" in French and refers to the Catholic missionaries who explored the area. Lake Champlain, in New York, is named for its discoverer, Samuel Champlain.

The French gave many descriptive names to places they discovered or founded. Boise, Idaho, comes from the French word for "woods." Presque Isle, in Pennsylvania, Maine, and Michigan, means "almost an island." Eau Claire, Wisconsin, means "clear water"; Fond du Lac, in Wisconsin and Minnesota, means "far end of the lake"; and Belle Plaine, Iowa, means "beautiful plain."

The word **ville** in French means "city" or "town." As with the word **town** in Jamestown and Englishtown, the word **ville** was added to another word to come up with the name of towns: Knoxville and Nashville in Tennessee; Belleville, La Fargeville, and Depauville in northern New York.

Italian, Greek, Latin, and German Influences

Spanish, English, French, and Indian words are the main sources of names of places in the United States, but there are others. America was named after the Italian explorer Amerigo Vespucci, who determined that the Americas were a separate continent from Asia.

Many American places were named after places and people of ancient Greek and Roman civilizations: Seneca, Ithaca, Carthage, Euclid. Philadelphia means "city of brotherly love" in Greek. Agricola, a town name in several states, means "farmer" in Latin. German settlers gave their new Missouri home a Latin name, Concordia, meaning "concord" or "peace."

Many cities in Pennsylvania end with the word **burg** or **burgh,** German for "castle" or "fort": Pittsburgh, Harrisburg, Strasburg, Mechanicsburg. Gothenburg, in Nebraska, the site of an old Pony Express station, was named for a city in Sweden.

Further Study

We could go on and on with the study of the origins of American place names. The richness and diversity of the population in the United States are evident in the great variety of place names. Remember, early settlers had an enormous new country to name. They used the languages and the names of places they knew. Settlers far away from home probably felt less homesick when surrounded by familiar place names.

When you see the name of a city or a street, a river or a lake, a state or a county, ask yourself what language it may have come from. You may find the origin and story of place names in dictionaries of American place names in your local or school library. Why don't you start by finding the story of the name of your street, city, county, or state?

Activity F

1. List three Spanish place names with their English meanings.

_____

2. Who lived in what is now the United States before any Europeans came?

_____

3. List three states with Indian names.

_____

4. Name three American cities that have been named for places in England.

_____

5. For whom is New York named?

_____

6. What do the French word **ville** and the German word **burg** mean? Can you find two cities in your area that end with **ville** and two that end with **burg?**

_____

7. List three French place names with their English meanings.

_____

8. What language does the name America come from?

_____

Resources and References

History of Language

Beowulf. Trans. Howell D. Chickering, Jr. Garden City, NY: Anchor Press/Doubleday, 1977.

Beowulf. Trans. Charles W. Kennedy. Eleventh Printing. New York: Oxford University Press, 1962.

Cahn, William, and Cahn, Rhoda. *The Story of Writing.* Harvey House, 1963.

Charlin, Remy; Beth, Mary; and Ancona, George. *Handtalk: An ABC of Finger Spelling and Sign Language.* Parents' Magazine Press, 1974.

Chaucer, Geoffrey. *The Riverside Chaucer.* Larry D. Benson, ed. Boston: Houghton Mifflin, 1987.

Davidson, Jessica. *Is That Mother in the Bottle? Where Language Came From and Where It Is Going.* New York: Watts, 1972.

Davidson, Marshall, ed. *Great Civilizations of the Past: Golden Book of Lost Worlds.* New York: Golden Books, 1962.

Epstein, Sam, and Epstein, Beryl. *All About Prehistoric Cave Men.* New York: Random House, 1959.

Ernst, Margaret. *Words: English Roots and How They Grew.* NY: Harper and Row, 1982.

Gannette, Henry. *The Origin of Certain Place Names in the United States.* Detroit: Gale Research Company, 1971.

Harder, Kelsie B. *Illustrated Dictionary of Place Names.* New York: Van Nostrand Reinhold, 1976.

Longman, Harold. *What's Behind the Word?* New York: Perl, Coward-McCann, 1968.

Pei, Mario. *The Story of Language.* Philadelphia: J.B. Lippincott, 1984.

Rogers, Frances. *Painted Rock to Printed Page: History of Printing and Communication.* Philadelphia: Lippincott, 1960.

Scott, Joseph, and Scott, Lenore. *Egyptian Hieroglyphs for Everyone: An Introduction to the Writing of Ancient Egypt.* New York: Funk and Wagnalls, 1968.

The World Book Encyclopedia. Chicago: World Book, Inc., 1994.

Foreign Countries

Balerdi, Susan. *France: The Crossroads of Europe.* Dillon Press, 1984. For younger readers.

Bradley, Catherine. *Germany: The Reunification of a Nation.* Gloucester Press, 1991. For younger readers.

Farfield, Sheila. *Peoples and Nations of Africa.* Gareth Stevens, 1988.

Georges, D.V. *South America.* Children's Press, 1986.

James, Ian. *Italy.* Watts, 1988. For younger readers.

Miller, Arthur. *Spain.* Chelsea House, 1988. For younger readers.

Resources and References *(continued)*

Filmstrips

Ancient Civilizations. National Geographic Society.
Christmas in France. Huntsville, TX: Educational Filmstrips.
Christmas in Germany. Huntsville, TX: Educational Filmstrips.
Christmas in Spain. Huntsville, TX: Educational Filmstrips.
France. Huntsville, TX: Educational Filmstrips.
Germany, West and East. Niles, IL: United Learning.
Glimpses of West Africa. Gessler Publishing Co.
Let's Visit Mexico. Pleasantville, NY: EAV.
Let's Visit South America. Pleasantville, NY: EAV.
Let's Visit Spain. Pleasantville, NY: EAV.
Martinique et Guadeloupe. Gessler Publishing Co.

Pedagogy

Curtain, A., and Pesola, Ann C. *Languages and Children—Making the Match.* Addison-Wesley, 1988.

Kennedy, D., and De Lorenzo, W.E. *Complete Guide to Exploratory Foreign Language Programs.* Lincolnwood, IL: National Textbook Company, 1985.

Raven, P.T. *FLEX: A Foreign Language Experience.* ERIC Document No. ED 238 301, 1983.

Seelye, H. Ned. *Teaching Culture.* Lincolnwood, IL: National Textbook Co., 1984.

Dictionaries

(All Amsco School Publications, New York)

The New College French & English Dictionary, 1988.
The New College German & English Dictionary, 1981.
The New College Italian & English Dictionary, 1976.
The New College Latin & English Dictionary, 1994.
The New College Spanish & English Dictionary, 1987.

To the Student

You are about to embark on a journey of discovery — beginning to learn a new language spoken by millions of people around the world, FRENCH.

Learning French provides an opportunity to explore another language and culture. French may be one of several languages you will discover in this course. You can then select which language you will continue to study.

Whatever your goals, this book will be a fun beginning in exploring a special gift you have as a human being: the ability to speak a language other than your own. The more you learn how to communicate with other people, the better you will be able to live and work in the world around you.

In this book, you will discover the French language and the world where it is spoken. The French words and expressions you will learn have been limited so that you will feel at ease.

You will learn how to express many things in French: how to greet people, how to count, how to tell the day and month of the year, how to identify and describe many objects, and more.

You will use French to talk about yourself and your friends. You will practice with many different activities, like puzzles and word games, French songs, cartoons, and pictures. Some activities you will do with classmates or with the whole class. You will act out fun skits and conversations and sing French songs. You will learn about many interesting bits of French culture: school days, holidays, school and leisure time, name days, gestures, and sports.

You will also meet young Claude, who will be your guide on how to pronounce French words. Look for Claude's clues throughout this book and get a feel for the French language, its sounds, and its musical quality. You will also develop an ear for French, so listen carefully to your teacher and the cassettes.

You will quickly realize that learning a new language is not as hard as you might have imagined. Enjoy using it with your teacher and classmates. Try not to be shy or afraid of making mistakes when speaking: remember, the more you speak, the more you will learn. And you can even show off the French you learn to family, relatives, and friends. After all, learning a new language means talking with the rest of the world and with each other.

Now — on to French. **Bonne chance!**, which means *Good luck!*

— K.R.A.

Contents

France and the French Language

1

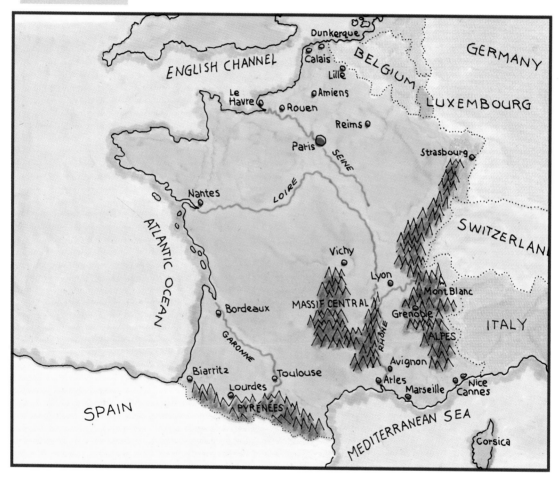

France, slightly smaller than the state of Texas, is the largest country in western Europe. Situated at the western edge of the European continent, France is shaped roughly like a hexagon, a six-sided figure. In fact, the French refer to their country as **l'hexagone**. Three of its sides border on water: the Mediterranean Sea, the Atlantic Ocean, and the English Channel. The other three sides border on land: Spain, Italy, Switzerland, Germany, Luxembourg, and Belgium.

NOTE TO TEACHERS

➡ Be sure not to rush through the introduction or the cultural sections, **En France**. Students are always intrigued by foreign lands and cultures. They ask many questions about cultural differences and remember cultural details long after they may have forgotten language and grammatical points.

➡ Take time to study the art and maps in the book and supplement the text with French postcards and magazines, travel brochures, posters, souvenirs and artifacts, slides and photographs, video materials, and so on. You may have students find some of these materials themselves. Relatives, friends, libraries, travel agencies, French consulates and cultural entities are excellent sources for students to contact. Set up a classroom bulletin board or have students create a collage in the shape of France and francophone countries on which to display postcards, photos, and so on.

➡ Students also love to hear personal stories and anecdotes. If possible, provide authentic and personalized information about French and francophone culture by relating your own stories or inviting a native or someone who has visited a French-speaking country to speak to students and answer questions.

En France (Supplementary Culture)

➡ Compared to the United States, France is a very old country. Paintings of hunting scenes in several caves in southwest France show that the area was inhabited as far back as prehistoric times. In the first century B.C., France was called **Gaul** and it already had a hero, **Vercingetorix**, who fought against the invading Roman armies. In the fifth century, the country took the name of **France.** The capital of France, **Paris**, was founded with the name **Lutèce** more than two thousand years ago on the Île de la Cité in the Seine river.

➡ Many great historical figures have contributed to the rich history of France.

- ◆ **Charlemagne,** the bearded emperor, organized schools for children around the year 800.

- ◆ **Jeanne d'Arc,** a young peasant girl, brought back courage to the French armies and helped free France from the invading English armies in 1412.

- ◆ **Henri IV,** "the good King Henri," lived around 1600 and wanted to see a chicken in the pot of every French family for its Sunday meal.

➡ In the sixteenth and seventeenth centuries, French explorers set out from Brittany to discover the world.

- ◆ 1534—**Jacques Cartier** took possession of Canada in the name of the king of France.

- ◆ 1608—**Samuel de Champlain** founded Quebec. Canada, called New France by the French, was lost to England in 1763.

- ◆ 1682—**Cavelier de La Salle** took possession of the Mississippi region and called it Louisiana in honor of the king of France, Louis XIV. In 1803, it became the property of the United States.

➡ During the nineteenth century, France acquired a vast colonial empire. Many countries in Africa and Asia became French colonies, subject to French laws, institutions, economic policy and trade. During the 1950s and 1960s, most French colonies became independent countries. However, France continues to have strong economic and cultural influence. French is still spoken by many people and taught in the schools established by the French in the nineteenth century.

The geography of France is varied, with low-lying plains, plateaus, forests, and mountains. Europe's highest peak, Mont Blanc, is located in southeastern France. The country is crisscrossed by four major river systems and their interconnecting canals. As an important agricultural center, France produces most of the foods its people consume.

France, often called **"la douce France"** (sweet France), was formerly a great colonial power. Its explorers and traders took the French language to many parts of the world. Paris, called **"la ville-lumière"** (the city of light), is the capital of France and one of the world's most beautiful cities.

The French language, derived from Latin, is a Romance language, like Spanish, Italian, Portuguese, and Romanian. Written in the Roman alphabet, French belongs to the Indo-European family of languages. The letters are the same as those in the English alphabet, but they are pronounced much differently. For example, the word Paris, written the same in English, is pronounced without the final **s** sound. There are also many accent marks in French that affect the sounds and/or the meanings of words.

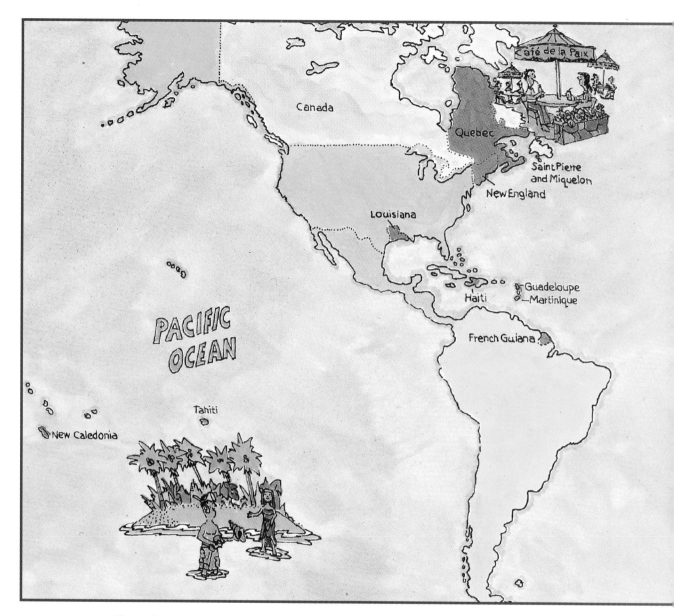

French is the official language of more than twenty countries around the world. Over one hundred million people speak French as their native language. In Europe, outside of France, French is spoken in Belgium, Luxembourg, Switzerland, and Monaco. On the American continent, French is the official language of three islands in the Caribbean: Haiti, Martinique, and Guadeloupe. Quebec, Canada's largest province, is almost entirely French-speaking. In the United States, French is a second language for more than a million people in Louisiana and certain areas of Vermont, New Hampshire, and Maine.

En France (continued)

➡ You may wish to point out that French-speaking countries vary enormously in size, climate, lifestyle, and spoken languages.

- ◆ In size, they range from Monaco, barely one-half square mile, to Zaire, more than 906,000 square miles.

- ◆ In climate, they range from the tropical rain forests of Zaire to the Sahara Desert in Algeria and the cold snowy winters of Canada.

- ◆ In lifestyle, they range from a very urbanized country like Belgium to an almost entirely rural and undeveloped country like Burkina Faso. Villages and cities are also very different, as are the houses people live in. In some countries, houses are as modern as those in the United States or France; in others, houses are made of sun-dried mud bricks and thatched roofs. Clothing may be western in style, or traditional, especially in rural areas.

- ◆ The people of some francophone countries speak French as well as one or more other languages.

  In Quebec, Canada, for example, 96 percent of the people speak French, while in the rest of Canada, only 24 percent speak French. Throughout Canada, traffic signs, advertising displays, directions on products, names of streets, and so on are written in both English and French. Schools in Quebec teach in French, and most schools elsewhere teach in English. Canadian universities use either French or English, and some are bilingual.

  In Luxembourg, elementary schools teach in German and high schools teach in French.

  In Switzerland 25 percent of the population, mostly located in the eastern part of the country, speak French, and schools in that area use French as the teaching language.

  In the four overseas departments of France—La Réunion, Guadeloupe, Martinique, and French Guiana—the school system, as well as all other institutions, use French as the standard language. Many people also speak a local patois or dialect.

NOTE TO TEACHERS

➡ Have students learn more about France and French-speaking countries by doing research projects, either as written or oral reports.

- ◆ Topics for research may involve choosing a French-speaking country, finding its size, population, capital city, bordering countries, language(s) spoken besides French, colors of the flag (see Note to Teachers, page 44), currency used, typical foods and dishes, holidays, dress styles, and so on. Prepare guiding questions to focus students' attention on the topics chosen.

- ◆ Have students bring maps, photographs from travel brochures or magazines, authentic photographs taken by friends or relatives, souvenirs, and music.

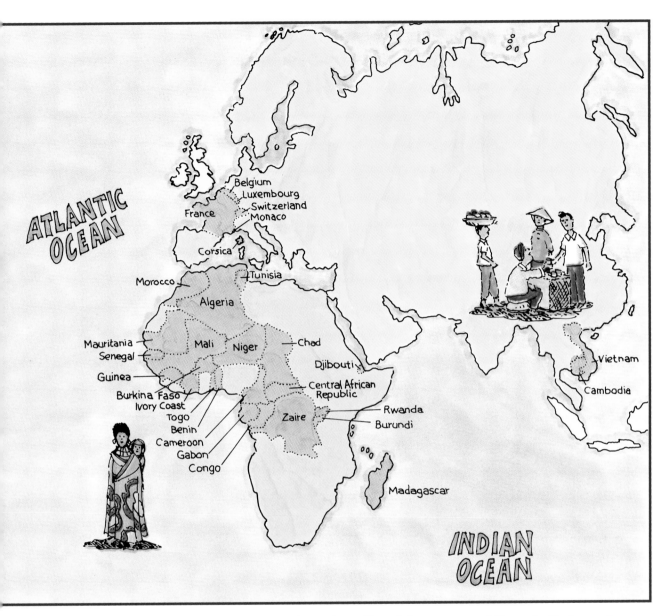

In South America, French is the official language of French Guiana. In Africa, France built a great colonial empire toward the end of the nineteenth century. French is still the official or second language in many African countries that were once French colonies: Algeria, Tunisia, Morocco, Senegal, Cameroon, Zaire, the Ivory Coast, and several other countries. These countries retain not only the French language but also the influence of French culture, institutions, and traditions. In Asia, the countries of Laos, Cambodia, and Vietnam (formerly Indochina) were also at one time French colonies, and French is still spoken today by some of its people.

Although English has now surpassed French as the language of international commerce, French is still one of the chief languages of diplomacy. It is one of the five official languages of the United Nations, and much of the information in American passports is written in French as well as English.

You may already be familiar with one of the best-known works of French literature, *Les Misérables*. Victor Hugo, a French writer, wrote this long novel early in the nineteenth century, and it is the basis for the modern musical that bears its name.

Did you know that French soldiers helped the United States win the Revolutionary War, that the Statue of Liberty was a gift from France on the occasion of the 100th anniversary of the American Revolution, and that a Frenchman designed our nation's capital, Washington, D.C.?

French cooking ranks very high among the world's cuisines. (The word **cuisine** means kitchen/cooking in French.) Crêpes, croissants, and omelettes are tasty examples of French food. Many English food words come from French: **mouton** = *mutton*, **bœuf** = *beef*, and **porc** = *pork*.

Now you have the opportunity to study this beautiful and influential language. Have fun and enjoy it.

En France (continued)

➡ There are at least two thousand newspapers and magazines published outside of France—most of them in Switzerland, Canada, and North Africa. There are also French-language high schools throughout the world. Radio programs in French, transmitted by the French radio station Radio France Internationale, can be heard all over the world.

➡ French literature has been influential throughout history. Several eighteenth-century writers, Montesquieu, Voltaire, Rousseau, and Diderot, inspired the writers of the American Constitution.

➡ You may wish to familiarize students with the variety of foods and dishes of the French-speaking world:

- **Couscous** from North Africa: steamed grain with vegetables and meat, usually lamb, served with a hot sauce.
- **Tajine** from Morocco and Tunisia: lamb, mutton, or chicken stewed with vegetables in an earthenware dish.
- Avocado stuffed with shrimp boiled with garlic, served cold, from Cameroon.
- **Mwab** from Zaire: chicken prepared with peanut butter. Also a manioc meal made from cassava and served with a spicy sauce.
- Goose liver from France.
- **Crêpe suzette** from France: dessert pancake with orange flavoring served flaming with an orange-flavored liqueur.
- Cheese fondue from Switzerland: melted cheese with wine into which French bread is dipped.
- **Carbonade** from Belgium: a beef stew cooked in beer.
- **Tourtière** from Canada: a meat pie.
- Fried pork served with fried bananas from Haiti.
- Spicy soup made with the meat of the conch from Martinique.

➡ In France, lunch is as important a meal as dinner, although dinner tends to be lighter. In some African francophone countries, the only meal of the day is a large dinner.

ANSWERS TO ACTIVITÉ

1. *France is the largest country in western Europe.*
2. *French, Spanish, Italian, Portuguese, and Romanian*
3. *Letters are the same, but they are pronounced very differently.*
4. *more than twenty countries*
5. *more than one hundred million people*
6. *Belgium, Luxembourg, Switzerland, and Monaco*
7. *Haiti, Martinique, and Guadeloupe*
8. *Louisiana and areas of Vermont, New Hampshire, and Maine*
9. *Africa*
10. *Victor Hugo*
11. *Both came from France.*

1. How does France compare with other European countries in size?

   _____

2. Name the Romance languages.

   _____

3. How does the French alphabet compare with the English alphabet?

   _____

4. How many countries retain French as their official language?

   _____

5. How many people throughout the world speak French as their native

   language? _____

6. In which European countries is French spoken?

   _____

7. Name three islands in the Caribbean where French is spoken.

   _____

8. Name the states in the United States where French is the second language.

   _____

9. Which continent has the greatest number of French-speaking countries?

   _____

10. Who wrote the novel entitled *Les Misérables*? _____

11. What do the Statue of Liberty and croissants have in common?

   _____

2 *French Cognates*

You already know many French words. Some of the words are spelled exactly like English words. In many other words, the only difference between English and French is an accent mark on one or two letters. One clue to watch for is the circumflex accent, which often occurs in a French word over a vowel that in English is followed by *s*: **hôpital** = *hospital*, **forêt** = *forest*. Also, words ending in *-er* in English frequently end in **-re** in French: **centre** = *center*, **décembre** = *December*. Words ending in *-y* in English often end in **-é** in French: **nationalité** = *nationality*, **réalité** = *reality*.

How many of the following French words can you recognize? Fill in the blanks with the English meanings. If you need to, you may look in a dictionary. Listen to your teacher or the cassette for the pronunciation of these words:

1. aéroport _____

2. américain _____

3. ancêtre _____

4. appartement _____

5. armée _____

6. arriver _____

7. art _____

8. autobus _____

9. automobile _____

10. banane _____

11. bleu _____

12. carotte _____

13. centre _____

14. céréale _____

15. certainement _____

16. charmant _____

17. chocolat _____

18. classe _____

19. décembre _____

20. dîner _____

NOTE TO TEACHERS

➡   Cognates provide a perfect opportunity to delight students with early discovery of words they can easily associate with what they already know.

➡   Point out to students that many English words come from French. Show them the following endings of English words, which generally indicate words borrowed from French:

- ◆ words ending in *-et*   ballet, bouquet, sorbet
- ◆ words ending in *-é*   café, fiancé, cliché, attaché case
- ◆ words ending in *-age*   garage, corsage, marriage, heritage

Have students find other English words ending in *-et, -é*, and *-age* such as: gourmet, cachet, filet, valet; blasé, consommé, emigré, entrée, passé, protégé, résumé, soufflé, toupee; entourage, mirage, bon voyage.

ANSWERS TO ACTIVITÉ

1. *airport*
2. *American*
3. *ancestor*
4. *apartment*
5. *army*
6. *arrive*
7. *art*
8. *bus*
9. *automobile*
10. *banana*
11. *blue*
12. *carrot*
13. *center*
14. *cereal*
15. *certainly*
16. *charming*
17. *chocolate*
18. *class*
19. *December*
20. *dinner*

ANSWERS *(continued)*

21. *electrician*
22. *family*
23. *geography*
24. *history*
25. *hospital*
26. *hotel*
27. *ideal*
28. *imagine*
29. *lion*
30. *liberty*
31. *May*
32. *mom*
33. *modern*
34. *model*
35. *music*
36. *national*
37. *nationality*
38. *uncle*
39. *person*
40. *poem*
41. *poet*
42. *problem*
43. *reality*

44. *salad*
45. *sandal*
46. *theater*
47. *tiger*
48. *timid*
49. *tourist*
50. *visit*

NOTE TO TEACHERS

You may want students to look at the illustration of advertisements on page 9 and guess the meanings of the French words that have English cognates.

21. électricien _____
22. famille _____
23. géographie _____
24. histoire _____
25. hôpital _____
26. hôtel _____
27. idéal _____
28. imaginer _____
29. lion _____
30. liberté _____
31. mai _____
32. maman _____
33. moderne _____
34. modèle _____
35. musique _____
36. national _____
37. nationalité _____
38. oncle _____
39. personne _____
40. poème _____
41. poète _____
42. problème _____
43. réalité _____

44. salade _____
45. sandale _____
46. théâtre _____
47. tigre _____
48. timide _____
49. touriste _____
50. visite _____

3 *French Names*

Now that you are able to recognize over 50 French words resembling English, let's look at how French and English names compare.

Claude is going to help you learn how to pronounce some of these names.

You will meet **Claude** throughout this book holding his lens over one or two pronunciation clues he wants to share with you as you develop a good French pronunciation.

Whenever you look at **Claude**'s clues, keep this in mind: every time you try to pronounce a French sound, hold your mouth, tongue, lips, and teeth in the same position at the end of the sound as you did at the beginning. Try saying **o** this way. Now try **oooo**. There, you've got it.

Claude has two clues for you before you listen to the following list of boys' and girls' names. These clues tell you how to pronounce HIS name:

au=oh

Claude

Pauline, Claudine

e at the end of a word is always silent.

final e

Claude, Marie

NOTE TO TEACHERS

➡ In each section, students encounter **Claude**, who will teach them pro-nunciation skills. Emphasize the phonetic concepts **Claude** presents. Model all French words for students and/or have them listen to the cassette. Have students repeat individually and in unison.

➡ To teach and practice the French sounds **Claude** presents in the book, you may wish to illustrate on cards two or three words containing the sounds introduced. Use the cards throughout the course to review sounds already studied.

➡ To have more fun with **Claude** and his clues, bring an oversized jacket and hat to class. Have students play **Claude**, wearing the jacket and hat as they model the sounds and words of **Claude's** clues to the class.

➡ Children love to be able to say the alphabet. You may reproduce the alphabet below for students and have the class repeat the alphabet several times, gaining speed with each repetition. You may also have students sing a familiar alphabet tune from nursery school, this time in French.

Letter	Name	Sound	Example
a	ah	*a* in *father*	**la** (*the*)
b	beh	*b* in *boy*	**bonjour** (*hello*)
c	seh	*ck* in *Dick* before *a, o, u* *c* in *cell* before *e, i,* and *y*	**content** (*glad*) **c'est** (*it is*)
d	deh	*d* in *day*	**dame** (*lady*)
e	eh	*e* in *quiet* *e* in *then* *e* in *they* *eu* in *uh*	**je** (*I*) **sept** (*seven*) **décembre** (*December*) **bleu** (*blue*)
f	effe	*f* in *fun*	**fille** (*girl*)
g	geh	*g* in *go* *s* in *pleasure*	**garçon** (*boy*) **garage** (*garage*)
h	hache	silent in French	**histoire** (*story*)
i	ih	*ee* in *meet*	**ici** (*here*)
j	ji	*s* in *pleasure*	**janvier** (*January*)
k	kah	*k* in *kiss*	**kilo** (*kilogram*)
l	elle	*l* in *like*	**livre** (*book*)
m	emme	*m* in *man*	**madame** (*madam*)

Alphabet *(continued)*

Letter	Name	Sound	Example
n	enne	*n* in *no*	**non** *(no)*
o	oh	*o* in *open*	**rose** *(rose)*
p	peh	*p* in *pin*	**père** *(father)*
q	ku	*c* in *music*	**quatre** *(four)*
r	erre	almost a gargle	**rouge** *(red)*
s	esse	*s* in *this*	**salon** *(living room)*
t	teh	*t* in *tall*	**table** *(table)*
u	uh	round lips as if about to whistle and say *ee* of *meet*	**une** *(a)*
v	veh	*v* in *voice*	**vingt** *(twenty)*
w	double veh	*v* in *voice* *w* in *week*	**wagon** *(wagon)* **week-end** *(weekend)*
x	ixe	*x* in *box*	**xylophone** *(xylophone)*
y	i grec	*y* in *yard*	**yeux** *(eyes)*
z	zede	*z* in *zebra*	**zéro** *(zero)*

▮ NOTE TO TEACHERS

➡ Have each student choose a French name. For additional names, students may consult the name day calendar on page 15. Here are the French boys' names on the list that do not resemble English, along with some English equivalents. Note that those girls' names that do not resemble English have no English equivalents:

Antoine	*Anthony*	**Guillaume**	*William*	**Michel**	*Michael*
Didier	*no equivalent*	**Jean**	*John*	**Pierre**	*Peter*
Étienne	*Steven*	**Laurent**	*Lawrence*	**René**	*no equivalent*
François	*Frank*	**Léon**	*Leo*	**Yves**	*no equivalent*
Gérard	*Gerald*	**Marcel**	*no equivalent*		

➡ Have students make name tags for the French names they have chosen. Students may write **Je m'appelle** before their French name.

Here is a list of boys' and girls' names. With your teacher's help, choose a French name that you would like to have for yourself while you are studying French:

Alain	Frédéric	Grégoire	Jacques	Laurent
Albert	Georges	Guillaume	Jean	Léon
Alexandre				Marc
André				Marcel
Antoine				Michel
Bernard				Nicolas
Bruno				Olivier
Charles				Paul
Claude				Philippe
Denis				Pierre
Didier				Raoul
Dominique				Raymond
Édouard				René
Étienne	Gérard	Guy	Joseph	Vincent
François	Gilbert	Henri	Julien	Yves

Adèle	Françoise	Isabelle	Madeleine	Michèle
Anne	Gabrielle	Jacqueline	Marguerite	Monique
Antoinette				Nathalie
Béatrice				Nicole
Bernadette				Patricia
Blanche				Pauline
Brigitte				Simone
Catherine				Solange
Cécile				Sophie
Chantal				Suzanne
Claire				Suzette
Claudine				Sylvie
Colette				Thérèse
Dominique				Véronique
Dorothée				Virginie
Élisabeth	Geneviève	Jeanne	Marie	Yolande
Estelle	Hélène	Lise	Marthe	Yvette

ACTIVITÉ

When the French want to say, "My name is Marie," they say, **"Je m'appelle Marie."** Practice telling your teacher and your classmates your name in French. If you and your teacher have chosen French names, use them.

Claude's clues:

Note to Teachers

➡ This **Activité** gives students immediate experience in using the language. If students have made French name tags, use them.

  ◆ Point to yourself and say, **"Je m'appelle _____ (your name)."**

  ◆ Then point to a student and ask, **"Comment t'appelles-tu?"** If the student does not understand, repeat your name. Model **"Je m'appelle"** again until the student catches on.

Repeat these two phrases with several students, giving as many as possible a chance to both ask and answer the question.

Remember, you can find the English equivalents of all French phrases in the final section, Vocabulary. All French materials are included in the cassette program.

➡ *Claude's clues:* Model pronunciation of the French **ç** and nasal **n** sounds for students. You may wish to refer students to the list of names on page 11 to find and pronounce additional words containing these sounds.

➡ Before students are asked to read Dialog 1 for meaning, have them look at the characters and guess what Pierre and Solange may be saying in each illustration.

➡ Next, model pronunciation either by reading aloud or by playing the cassette while students read the dialog.

➡ Have students close their books. Read short segments for students to repeat. If a phrase is too long, break it into shorter sections, reading the last part first. Have students repeat, then add another word or two until you have read the entire segment. Have students repeat after each addition. For example:

> **t'appelles-tu?**
> **comment t'appelles-tu?**
> **Et toi, comment t'appelles-tu?**

➡ Ask questions:

- How do the boy and girl say hello?
- What does the girl ask the boy?
- What is the boy's name?
- Are they happy to meet each other?
- What do they say to each other?
- How do they say good-bye?

➡ To help students understand that French is a very musical language, teach some intonation patterns. Have students listen to the cassette for examples of the following intonation patterns:

- In normal conversation, the pitch of the voice rises higher and descends lower than in English.
- In short declarative sentences, the voice usually rises during the first part and descends during the second: In **"Je m'appelle Solange,"** **"je m'appelle"** rises and **"Solange"** descends.
- In longer sentences, each segment usually rises with the last part dropping: **"Moi, je m'appelle Pierre, et toi, tu t'appelles Solange."**
- Questions that can be answered yes or no rise: **"Ça va?"**
- Questions that require information descend: **"Comment t'appelles-tu?"**

Dialog 1 *Bonjour*

* **tu** means *you* in French; **tu** is used when you are speaking to a close rela-
tive, a friend, or a child — someone with whom you are familiar. To say
you, the French also use **vous** when speaking to a stranger or a grown-
up — a person with whom you should be formal. The exercises in this
book use **tu** and its related forms **toi** and **te** (**t'**).

ACTIVITÉ

Now let's review what you learned in Dialog 1:

1. Bonjour, _____ (name).

Bonjour, _____ (name).

2. Comment t'appelles-tu?

Je m'appelle _____.

3. Enchanté, _____ (name).

Enchantée,* _____ (name).

4. Au revoir.

Au revoir.

* Did you notice in Dialog 1 that Pierre says **Enchanté** and Solange says **Enchantée**? The reason is that French nouns and adjectives, unlike English, have gender. They are either masculine or feminine. An **e** is often added to the masculine form to make it feminine.

➡ Introduce the words **monsieur, madame, mademoiselle** on the chalk-board by writing the words before names of people students know. Model pronunciation for the class.

➡ Greet students and ask them to respond by greeting you with **"Bonjour, monsieur (madame, mademoiselle)."**

➡ Tell students your name, then ask theirs. Have students ask their classmates their names.

➡ Circulate among students, shaking hands with them as you say, **"Enchanté(e) monsieur (mademoiselle) ____** (last name)" and they reply, **"Enchanté(e) monsieur (madame, mademoiselle) ____** (your name)." They could then proceed to shake hands with each other. Occasionally ask students whether **enchanté** takes one **e** or two.

➡ Explain to students that whenever the French greet someone whose name they do not know, the greeting is generally followed by **monsieur, madame,** or **mademoiselle**. For example, when entering a shop, say, **"Bonjour, madame"** to a female clerk. When leaving, say, **"Au revoir, madame."**

➡ In pairs, have students practice the vocabulary of Dialog 1. Challenge students to improvise a skit in front of the class between two people who have just met, ending with **"Au revoir, monsieur (madame, mademoiselle)."**

➡ Note that the optional dialog, Dialog 4, **"Bonsoir,"** introducing **vous**, is included on page 53 of the Teacher Annotations. You may reproduce it for your students if you wish to teach the **vous** form. Introduce Dialog 4 at the end of Section 10, "Talking About Yourself."

En France (Supplementary Culture)

➡ You may wish to help students find their names or family members' names on the name day calendar. Ask students to find a friend or an acquaintance whom they can wish **Bonne Fête!**

➡ If the class includes students from different ethnic backgrounds, ask them if their families celebrate name days.

➡ Point out that compound names like **Marie-Claire, Jeanne-Marie, Jean-Paul,** and **Pierre-Henri** are very common French names. People with compound names usually celebrate their name day on the day of one of the saint's names, for example, **Marie-Hélène** is celebrated on August 18, the day of **Ste Hélène**. Ask students if compound names are popular in the United States and if they can think of a few examples, such as Anne Marie, Billy Joe, Betty Jane, Norma Jean, Peggy Sue.

➡ You may wish to explain to students that children are sometimes named after the saint commemorated on the day of their birth. Point out that some days on the calendar indicate the name of a holiday rather than the name of a saint. This may explain why in some French-speaking countries, the names **Fête Nat**, short for *Independence Day,* and **Toussaint**, *All Saints' Day,* are sometimes given to boys born on July 14 and November 1 respectively.

En France

Name Days

All children look forward to their special day, their birthday. French children are doubly lucky. They celebrate not only their birthday but also their name day. Most French names come from the names of saints. If you look at a French calendar, you will notice that each day is devoted to a different saint. On their name day, French children may receive presents and celebrate at an afternoon party with friends or at a special dinner with family. Everyone wishes them **Bonne Fête!** (*Happy Name Day!*)

When children become adults, more importance is given to celebrating name days than birthdays. Cards and flowers are always offered as presents and everyone knows when to wish you **Bonne Fête!**

#	JANVIER	FÉVRIER	MARS	AVRIL
1	J. de L'AN	se Ella	s Aubin	s Hugues
2	s Basile	Présentation	s Ch. le Bon	se Sandrine
3	se Geneviève	s Blaise	s Guénolé	s Richard
4	s Odilon	se Véronique	Carême	s Isidore
5	s Édouard	se Agathe	s Olive	se Irène
6	s Melaine	s Gaston	se Colette	s Marcellin
7	Épiphanie	se Eugénie	se Félicité	s J.B. de la S.
8	s Lucien	se Jacqueline	s Jean de D.	Rameaux
9	se Alix	se Apolline	se Franç R.	s Gautier
10	s Guillaume	s Arnaud	s Vivien	s Fulbert
11	s Paulin	N.-D. Lourdes	se Rosine	s Stanislas
12	se Tatiana	s Félix	se Justine	s Jules
13	se Yvette	se Béatrice	s Rodrigue	Vend. Saint
14	se Nina	s Valentin	se Mathilde	s Maxime
15	s Remi	s Claude	se Louise M.	PÂQUES
16	s Marcel	se Julienne	se Bénédicte	s Ben. J. L.
17	se Roseline	s Alexis	s Patrice	s Anicet
18	se Prisca	se Bernadette	s Cyrille	s Parfait
19	s Marius	s Gabin	s Joseph	se Emma
20	s Sébastien	se Aimée	s Herbert	se Odette
21	se Agnès	s P. Damien	se Clémence	s Anselme
22	s Vincent	se Isabelle	Mi-Carême	s Alexandre
23	s Barnard	s Lazare	s Victorien	s Georges
24	s Franç. Sales	s Modeste	Annonciat.	s Fidèle
25	Conv. s. Paul	s Roméo	s Humbert	s Marc
26	se Paule	s Nestor	s Larissa	se Alida
27	se Angèle	Mardi gras	s Habib	se Zita
28	s Th. D'Aquin	Cendres	s Gontran	se Valérie
29	s Gildas		se Gwladys	Souvenir Dép.
30	se Martine		s Amédée	s Robert
31	se Marcelle		s Benjamin	

#	MAI	JUIN	JUILLET	AOÛT
1	TRAVAIL	s Justin	s Thierry	s Alphonse
2	s Boris	se Blandine	s Martin	s Julien
3	ss Phil./Jacq.	PENTECÔTE	s Thomas	se Lydie
4	s Sylvain	se Clotilde	s Florent	s JM Vianney
5	se Judith	s Igor	s Ant.-Marie	s Abel
6	se Prudence	s Norbert	se Marietta G.	Transfig.
7	se Gisèle	s Gilbert	s Raoul	s Gaétan
8	Victoire 1945	s Médard	s Thibaut	s Dominique
9	s Pacôme	se Diane	se Amand.	s Amour
10	se Solange	s Landry	s Ulrich	s Laurent
11	se Estelle	s Barnabé	s Benoît	se Claire
12	s Achille	s Guy	s Olivier	se Clarisse
13	Fête J. d'Arc	s Ant. de Pa.	ss Henri/Joël	s Hippol.
14	s Matthias	s Élisée	FÊTE NAT.	s Evrard
15	se Denise	se Germaine	s Donald	ASSOMPT.
16	s Honoré	s J.F. Régis	ND Mt. Car.	s Armel
17	s Pascal	Dieu/Pères	se Charlotte	s Hyacinthe
18	s Éric	s Léonce	s Frédéric	se Hélène
19	s Yves	s Romuald	s Arsène	s Jean Eudes
20	s Bernardin	s Silvère	se Marina	s Bernard
21	s Constant.	s Rudolphe	s Victor	s Christophe
22	s Émile	Sacré-Coeur	se Marie-Mad.	s Fabrice
23	s Didier	se Audrey	se Brigitte	s Rose
24	ASCENSION	s Jean-Bapt.	se Christine	s Barthélemy
25	se Sophie	s Prosper	s Jac. le Maj.	s Louis
26	s Bérenger	s Anthelme	s Anne	se Natache
27	F. des Mères	s Fernand	se Nathalie	se Monique
28	s Germain	s Irénée	s Samson	s Augustin
29	s Aymar	ss Pierre/Paul	se Marthe	se Sabine
30	s Ferdinand	s Martial	se Juliette	s Fiacre
31	Visitation		s Ignace de L.	s Aristide

#	SEPTEMBRE	OCTOBRE	NOVEMBRE	DÉCEMBRE
1	s Gilles	se Thér. EJ	TOUSSAINT	se Florence
2	se Ingrid	s Léger	Défunts	Avent
3	s Grégoire	s Gérard	s Hubert	s Fr.-Xavier
4	se Rosalie	s Franç. d'As.	s Charles Bo.	se Barbara
5	se Raissa	se Fleur	se Sylvie	s Gérald
6	s Bertrand	s Bruno	se Bertille	s Nicolas
7	se Reine	s Serge	se Carine	s Ambroise
8	Nativité N-D	se Pélagie	s Geoffroy	Imm. Conc.
9	s Alain	s Denis	s Théodore	s P. Fourier
10	se Inès	s Ghislain	s Léon	s Romaric
11	s Adelphe	s Firmin	Vict. 1918	s Daniel
12	s Apollinaire	s Wilfried	s Christian	se JF de Chant.
13	s Aimé	s Géraud	s Brice	se Lucie
14	Sainte Croix	s Juste	s Sidoine	se Odile
15	s Roland	se Thér. A	s Albert	s Ninon
16	se Édith	se Edwige	se Marguerite	se Alice
17	s Renaud	s Baudouin	se Élisabeth	s Judicaël
18	se Nadège	s Luc	se Aude	s Gatien
19	se Émilie	s René	s Tanguy	s Urbain
20	s Davy	se Adeline	s Edmond	s Théophile
21	s Matthieu	se Céline	Présent. N-D	s P. Canisius
22	s Maurice	se Salomé	se Cécile	se Fr.-Xavière
23	s Constant	s Jean de Ca.	s Clément	s Armand
24	se Thècle	s Florentin	se Flora	se Adèle
25	s Hermann	s Crépin	se Cath. Lab.	NOËL
26	ss Côme/Dam.	s Dimitri	se Delphine	s Étienne
27	s Vinc. de P.	se Émeline	s Séverin	s Jean Apôt.
28	s Venceslas	s Simon	s Jacq. de M.	ss Innocents
29	s Michel	s Narcisse	s Saturnin	s David
30	s Jérôme	s Bienvenue	s André	Ste Famille
31		s Quentin		s Sylvestre

4 *Numbers*

Claude's clues:

r = almost a gargle

French **r** is pronounced at the back of the throat almost like a gargle.

é
et } = eh
final
er

tigre, liberté   enchanté, aéroport, Olivier, et

You will soon be able to count to forty in French.
Listen to your teacher or the cassette to learn how
to say the numbers 1 to 20.

1 un 2 deux 3 trois 4 quatre 5 cinq 6 six
7 sept 8 huit 9 neuf 10 dix 11 onze 12 douze 13 treize
14 quatorze 15 quinze 16 seize 17 dix-sept 18 dix-huit 19 dix-neuf 20 vingt

NOTE TO TEACHERS

➡ *Claude's clues:* Model pronunciation of the French **r** and **é** sounds for students. For additional practice words, refer to the list of cognates on pages 8 and 9, or the list of names on page 11.

➡ Model pronunciation of all numbers from 1 to 10, allowing time for repetition:

♦ **un / deux / trois** and so on.

➡ Have students repeat groups of numbers:

♦ **un, deux, trois / quatre, cinq, six / sept, huit, neuf, dix**

♦ **un, deux, trois, quatre, cinq / six, sept, huit, neuf, dix**

♦ **dix, neuf, huit, sept, six, cinq, quatre, trois, deux, un**

♦ **deux, quatre, six, huit, dix / un, trois, cinq, sept, neuf**

➡ **Combien?** = *How many?* Hold up one finger, then two, then three, and so on. Each time, ask, **"Combien?"** allowing the whole class time to respond.

➡ Model pronunciation of numbers 11 through 20: **onze / douze / treize** and so on.

➡ Have students repeat these numbers in groups as above.

➡ Count from **un** to **vingt** with even numbers, then with odd.

➡ As a listening comprehension activity, have each student write her or his telephone number, real or made up, on a piece of paper. Students then drop the telephone numbers into a box. Choose a student to pick a number from the box and read it aloud in French to the class. As soon as the telephone number is recognized, the student yells out: **"C'est à moi"** *(It's mine).* That student then picks another number from the box and reads it aloud to the class.

➡ Indicate items in the classroom: the teacher, light(s), desk, books on the desk, doors, windows, pencils, girls, boys. After pointing to each object or group of objects, query, **"Combien?"**

➡ As a vocabulary study aid for students, you may wish to duplicate the format of this first **Activité** in each of the following sections. List French words to be learned in the left column followed by blank rules. List English equivalents in the right column. Illustrations may substitute English equivalents.

➡ Have students write the numbers they hear, stopping after every four numbers to check answers:

ANSWERS TO ACTIVITÉ *(teacher dictation in brackets)*

1. [treize] *13*	**5.** [un] *1*	**9.** [douze] *12*
2. [quatre] *4*	**6.** [dix-huit] *18*	**10.** [onze] *11*
3. [dix-neuf] *19*	**7.** [cinq] *5*	**11.** [seize] *16*
4. [dix-sept] *17*	**8.** [quinze] *15*	**12.** [vingt] *20*

➡ Here is a simple song students will enjoy to learn the numbers one to twenty. To practice all the numbers up to twenty, change numbers in song to odd, then even numbers. Use two numbers only in each of the last two lines.

Un, Deux, Trois, Nous Irons au Bois

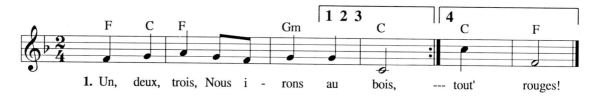

1. Un, deux, trois, Nous irons au bois, --- tout' rouges!

2. Quatre, cinq, six, cueillir des cerises,
3. Sept, huit, neuf, dans un panier neuf,
4. Dix, onze, douze, elles seront tout' rouges!

Translation   ONE, TWO, THREE, WE WILL GO TO THE WOODS
    1. One, two, three, we will go to the woods.
    2. Four, five, six, pick some cherries,
    3. Seven, eight, nine, in a new basket,
    4. Ten, eleven, twelve, they will be all red!

1. Cover page 16 with a sheet of paper. Then cover the French number words below and say the numbers aloud in French.
2. Now cover the French number words and write the French number words in the blank lines.

onze	_____	11	trois	_____	3
dix-huit	_____	18	huit	_____	8
quinze	_____	15	un	_____	1
cinq	_____	5	quatorze	_____	14
douze	_____	12	six	_____	6
sept	_____	7	deux	_____	2
dix-neuf	_____	19	neuf	_____	9
dix	_____	10	treize	_____	13
vingt	_____	20	seize	_____	16
quatre	_____	4	dix-sept	_____	17

3. Pretend you are the teacher and correct your work with a red pen or pencil. You will be able to see at a glance which words you need to study further.

Your teacher will read some French numbers to you. Write the numerals for the number you hear:

1._____   4._____   7._____   10._____

2._____   5._____   8._____   11._____

3._____   6._____   9._____   12._____

Let's continue learning numbers. Listen to your teacher or the cassette to learn how to say the numbers 21 to 40.

ACTIVITÉ

Cover the top of page 18 with a sheet of paper while you do the next three activities. Your teacher will read some numbers from 21 to 40 in random order to you. Write the numerals for the French number you hear:

1. _____   6. _____

2. _____   7. _____

3. _____   8. _____

4. _____   9. _____

5. _____   10. _____

NOTE TO TEACHERS

➡ Model pronunciation of numbers 21 to 30, allowing time for repetition. Ask students if they see a pattern in the numbers 21 to 30.

➡ After they point out the pattern, ask them to try to compose the numbers 31 to 39 aloud.

➡ Now model pronunciation of numbers 31 to 40, allowing time for repetition.

➡ Have students repeat groups of numbers sequentially, even, and odd, forward and then backward.

➡ Have students repeat numbers 20 to 40 in multiples of 2 and 5, forward and then backward.

➡ For additional review, write a French number word on a piece of paper for each student in the class. Distribute numbers at random. Have students line up in the correct number order. Once lined up, have students yell out their numbers in sequence.

➡ For authentic practice in writing number words, distribute copies of blank checks with a dollar amount from 1 to 40 written in digits. Have students complete the checks by writing the dollar amount in words.

➡ Have students write the numbers they hear, stopping after every five numbers to check answers.

ANSWERS TO ACTIVITÉ *(teacher dictation in brackets)*

1. [vingt]	*20*		**6.** [trente-trois]	*33*
2. [quarante]	*40*		**7.** [vingt-quatre]	*24*
3. [trente]	*30*		**8.** [vingt-huit]	*28*
4. [vingt et un]	*21*		**9.** [trente-six]	*36*
5. [trente et un]	*31*		**10.** [vingt-sept]	*27*

ANSWERS TO ACTIVITÉ

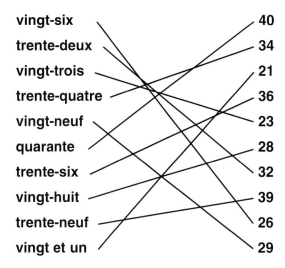

vingt-six	40
trente-deux	34
vingt-trois	21
trente-quatre	36
vingt-neuf	23
quarante	28
trente-six	32
vingt-huit	39
trente-neuf	26
vingt et un	29

Have students write the French number words for the numbers they hear, stopping after every five numbers to check answers.

ANSWERS TO ACTIVITÉ *(teacher dictation in brackets)*

1. [thirty-two] **trente-deux**

2. [twenty-three] **vingt-trois**

3. [thirty-seven] **trente-sept**

4. [twenty-nine] **vingt-neuf**

5. [twenty-six] **vingt-six**

6. [thirty-four] **trente-quatre**

7. [thirty-eight] **trente-huit**

8. [twenty-two] **vingt-deux**

9. [thirty-nine] **trente-neuf**

10. [twenty-five] **vingt-cinq**

See how many French number words you can recognize. Draw a line to match the French number word with its numeral:

vingt-six	40
trente-deux	34
vingt-trois	21
trente-quatre	36
vingt-neuf	23
quarante	28
trente-six	32
vingt-huit	39
trente-neuf	26
vingt et un	29

Now your teacher will read some numbers in English. Write the number words in French:

1. _____   6. _____

2. _____   7. _____

3. _____   8. _____

4. _____   9. _____

5. _____   10. _____

Now that you know the numbers from 1 to 40, let's try some math. First let's look at some words you will need to know:

dix **et** huit **font** dix-huit   10 + 8 = 18

dix-neuf **moins** sept **font** douze   19 − 7 = 12

Now write the answers to the following arithmetic problems in French. Then find the correct answers in the puzzle. Circle them from left to right, right to left, up or down, or diagonally:

1. trente-deux moins vingt-deux font _____

2. dix-neuf moins deux font _____

3. neuf et sept font _____

4. quinze et quinze font _____

5. vingt et vingt font _____

6. onze moins sept font _____

7. quatorze moins deux font _____

8. vingt-deux et trois font _____

9. trente-huit moins vingt font _____

10. vingt-sept et douze font _____

11. quinze et cinq font _____

12. sept et sept font _____

Here is a song students can enjoy while practicing the numbers 1 to 40. You may wish to use only numbers from 20 to 40 or multiples of 2 or 5.

Un Kilomètre à Pied

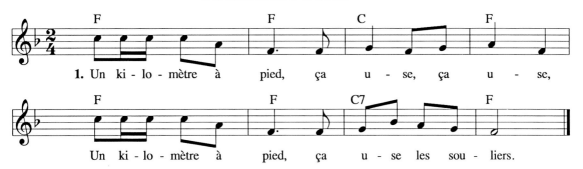

1. Un ki - lo - mètre à pied, ça u - se, ça u - se,
   Un ki - lo - mètre à pied, ça u - se les sou - liers.

2. Deux kilomètres à pied, ça dure, ça dure,
   Deux kilomètres à pied, ça dure un jour entier.

3. Trois kilomètres à pied, ça m'laisse, ça m'laisse,
   Trois kilomètres à pied, ça m'laisse fatigué[e].

Translation   *1 KILOMETER ON FOOT*

1. *One kilometer on foot, that wears, that wears,*
   One kilometer on foot, that wears out the shoes.

2. *Two kilometers on foot, that lasts, that lasts,*
   Two kilometers on foot, that lasts a whole day long.

3. *Three kilometers on foot, that makes me, that makes me,*
   Three kilometers on foot, that makes me tired.

NOTE TO TEACHERS

➡ If this Activité is done in class, check answers to math problems before students begin the word search. Note: Answers to puzzle on page 21.

➡ Tell students that accents on capital letters may be omitted for this and all other puzzles in the book.

ANSWERS TO ACTIVITÉ

1. *dix*
2. *dix-sept*
3. *seize*
4. *trente*
5. *quarante*
6. *quatre*
7. *douze*
8. *vingt-cinq*
9. *dix-huit*
10. *trente-neuf*

11. *vingt*
12. *quatorze*
13. *quinze*
14. *treize*
15. *trente et un*
16. *sept*
17. *trente-trois*
18. *vingt et un*
19. *onze*
20. *dix-neuf*

13. vingt-trois moins huit font _____

14. sept et six font _____

15. sept et vingt-quatre font _____

16. douze moins cinq font _____

17. vingt-six et sept font _____

18. quarante moins dix-neuf font _____

19. seize moins cinq font _____

20. vingt-six moins sept font _____

```
I   V   I   N   G   T   C   I   N   Q   F   U   E   E
L   I   A   Q   U   A   R   A   N   T   E   I   X   Z
T   N   Z   M   Z   Q   U   A   T   R   E   D   D   R
I   G   D   D   O   P   F   Q   S   E   F   I   H   O
U   T   C   R   F   N   A   H   U   X   X   X   A   T
H   Y   D   I   X   S   E   P   T   N   L   K   R   A
X   N   U   T   E   E   T   N   E   R   T   E   M   U
I   E   Z   I   E   S   S   U   E   Z   N   I   U   Q
D   U   Q   R   A   I   F   Q   X   T   D   N   D   E
N   O   G   L   F   U   E   N   E   T   N   E   R   T
P   N   P   Z   A   H   C   I   Q   G   S   R   X   I
E   Z   U   O   D   V   I   N   G   T   E   T   U   N
K   E   Z   I   E   R   T   K   L   N   P   O   R   U
S   I   O   R   T   E   T   N   E   R   T   Y   A   X
```

5 Days of the Week

Claude's clues:

a alone
= ah

mardi, samedi

i alone
= ee
of meet

jeudi, vendredi

NOVEMBRE

lundi	mardi	mercredi	jeudi	vendredi	samedi	dimanche
1	2	3	4	5	6	7
8	9	10	11	12	13	14
15	16	17	18	19	20	21
22	23	24	25	26	27	28
29	30	31				

These are the days of the week in French. The first letter is not capitalized. The French week begins with Monday.

C'est aujourd'hui lundi. = *Today is Monday.*

Each day, find as many people as you can and tell them the day of the week in French.

NOTE TO TEACHERS

➡ *Claude's clues:* Model pronunciation of the French **a** and **i** sounds for students.

➡ After drilling the days of the week with a wall calendar or calendar transparency, have students take turns greeting the class with, **"Bonjour, classe. C'est aujourd'hui _____."**

➡ At the beginning of each class period, have a different student greet the class, say the day of the week, and write it on the chalkboard.

➡ Here is a song to practice the days of the week. You may wish to give the English meanings for new words in the song before starting to sing.

Bonjour Lundi

Bon - jour lun - di!   Com -ment va mar - di?   Très bien, mer - cre - di.

Va dire à jeu - di   s'il voit ven -dre -di   a - vec sa - me - di,   Qu'on vien-dra di- man -che.

Translation

GOOD MORNING MONDAY

Good morning Monday!
How is Tuesday?
Very well, Wednesday.
Go tell Thursday
if he sees Friday
with Saturday
that we'll come on Sunday.

En France (Supplementary Culture)

Students may be interested in comparing French and American school systems. You may wish to present all or part of the following points.

➡ Schools in France consist of the following levels:

◆ **Primary School**
Nursery school and Kindergarten: children two to six years old.
Elementary school, grades 1 to 5: children six to ten years old.

◆ **Secondary School**

Middle school, grades 6 to 9: students eleven to fourteen years old.

High school: In grades 8 and 9, students' academic performance is evaluated. According to the evaluation results, students are placed either in a vocational high school **(lycée professionnel)** or a high school **(lycée)**.

The **lycée professionnel** prepares students for an apprenticeship or a job.

The **lycée** prepares students for a university education and a profession. At the end of the **lycée,** students take a difficult final examination that determines eligibility for admission to university. Only about 65 percent of students pass the exam and go on to university.

➡ Ask students which school and grade they would be attending if they lived in France.

École primaire *(Primary school)*

Âge	Classe	
6	cours primaire	*1st*
7	cours élémentaire 1	*2nd*
8	cours élémentaire 2	*3rd*
9	cours moyen 1	*4th*
10	cours moyen 2	*5th*

C.E.S. *(Middle school)*

Âge	Classe	
11	sixième	*6th*
12	cinquième	*5th*
13	quatrième	*4th*
14	troisième	*3rd*

Lycée *(High school)*

Âge	Classe	
15	seconde	*2nd*
16	première	*1st*
17	terminale	*last*

À l'école (At school)

Complete the following school schedule with the subjects you are taking this year:

	LUNDI	MARDI	MERCREDI	JEUDI	VENDREDI

Now look at a schedule of a French middle-school student. Compare it with yours. What are the differences? What are the similarities?

	LUNDI	MARDI	MERCREDI	JEUDI	VENDREDI	SAMEDI
8:00 – 9:00	Math	French	French	English	Math	French
9:00 – 10:00	Civics	Science	Readings from students' journals	French	History	Physical Education
10:00 – 10:30	Recreation	English	Music	Recreation	Recreation	Drawing
10:30 – 11:00	Drawing	Recreation	English	Geography	Library	English
11:00 – 12:00	French	History		Math	Science	
2:00 – 3:00	Technology	Physical Education		Chemistry	Music	
3:00 – 4:00	Class trip to mountain-climbing center	French		Civics	French	
4:00 – 5:00		Robotics		Chess Club		

School is taken very seriously in France. Many students do not finish their classes until 4, 5, or 6 o'clock in the evening, except on Wednesday and Saturday, when they have a half-day.

French report cards are distributed three times a year. Grades range from 1 to 20, with 10 being the passing grade and 15 or more a very good grade.

Parents of French students receive weekly reports on the progress of their children. Teachers and parents may write notes, information, questions, and comments to each other in a special notebook of correspondence that all students keep.

6 | *Months of the Year*

Claude's clues:

eu = uh

ille = ee-yuh

bl**eu**, j**eu**di, mons**ieur**

fam**ille**, ju**ille**t

The months of the year in French resemble English. Can you recognize all of them?

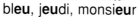

JANVIER

FÉVRIER

MARS

AVRIL

MAI

JUIN

JUILLET

AOÛT

SEPTEMBRE

OCTOBRE

NOVEMBRE

DÉCEMBRE

➡ *Claude's clues:* Model pronunciation of the French **eu** and **ille** sounds for students. Additional practice words may include:

♦ **neuf, dix-neuf, vingt-neuf, trente-neuf**

♦ **La jeune fille Camille arrive en Europe jeudi.**

➡ You may wish to use a wall calendar or transparency to introduce the names of the months.

➡ Drill the months by going up and down the rows, eliciting the names of the months sequentially **janvier** to **décembre** and then backward **décembre** to **janvier**. As students gain confidence, pick up speed.

ANSWERS TO ACTIVITÉ

1. F E V R I E R
2. A V R I L
3. M A I
4. J U I N
5. D E C E M B R E
6. M A R S
7. S E P T E M B R E
8. J A N V I E R
9. J U I L L E T
10. N O V E M B R E
11. A O U T
12. O C T O B R E

ACTIVITÉ

Unscramble the letters to form the name of a French month:

1. R R E E V F I

2. R L A I V

3. A I M

4. U J N I

5. B E C E D R M E

6. A S M R

7. T E S M P R E B E

8. R E J I V A N

9. L J E L U I T

10. O E E R N M V B

11. O T U A

12. T B C R O O E

Match the names of the months with their numbers by drawing lines between the two columns. For example, January is number one and December is number twelve:

août	cinq
avril	dix
décembre	douze
février	deux
janvier	neuf
juin	huit
juillet	quatre
mai	six
mars	sept
novembre	trois
octobre	onze
septembre	un

ANSWERS TO ACTIVITÉ

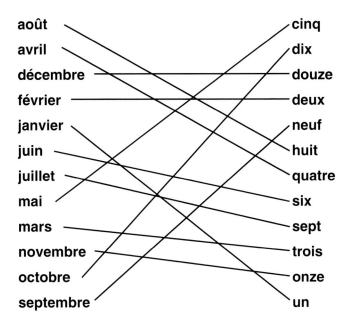

août	cinq
avril	dix
décembre	douze
février	deux
janvier	neuf
juin	huit
juillet	quatre
mai	six
mars	sept
novembre	trois
octobre	onze
septembre	un

Answers to Activité will vary.

 NOTE TO TEACHERS

➡ For the activities on pages 27 to 29, you may wish to introduce these simple expressions and have students answer with complete sentences:

- ◆ **C'est février . . .**   *It is February . . .*
  C'est lundi; c'est mardi . . .   *It is Monday; it is Tuesday . . .*
- ◆ **C'est en mars . . .**   *It is in March . . .*

➡ To practice the months of the year, students may enjoy singing a French version of the familiar "Thirty Days Has November."

Les Douze Mois

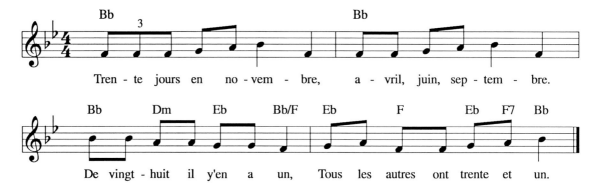

Translation   THE TWELVE MONTHS

Thirty days has November, April, June, and September.
Of twenty-eight there's only one. All the rest have thirty-one.

Answer the following questions with the French months:

1. Which is your favorite month?

   _____

2. Which is your least favorite month?

   _____

3. In which month is your birthday?

   _____

4. In which month does your mother celebrate her birthday?

   _____

5. In which month does your father celebrate his birthday?

   _____

6. In which month does your best friend celebrate her/his

   birthday? _____

7. When does your teacher celebrate her/his birthday?

   _____

8. In which months do you have vacation?

   _____

Fill in the blanks with the correct French names of the days or months, then find the nineteen names of the day or month in the puzzle. Circle them from left to right, right to left, up or down, or diagonally:

1. The first day of the week in France: _____

2. Many people go to church on this day of the week: _____

3. The day after Monday: _____

4. The last day of your school week: _____

5. The day after Tuesday: _____

6. The first day of the weekend: _____

7. The next to the last day of your school week: _____

8. The month of Valentine's Day: _____

9. Flag Day is celebrated in this month: _____

10. The first day of the new school year usually occurs in this month: _____

11. The month of Thanksgiving: _____

12. April Fool's Day is the first day of this month: _____

13. The month of Christmas: _____

14. The month of the United States' birthday: _____

15. The month after July: _____

ANSWERS TO ACTIVITÉ

1. *lundi*
2. *dimanche*
3. *mardi*
4. *vendredi*
5. *mercredi*
6. *samedi*
7. *jeudi*
8. *février*
9. *juin*
10. *septembre*
11. *novembre*
12. *avril*
13. *décembre*
14. *juillet*
15. *août*

ANSWERS TO ACTIVITÉ *(continued)*

16. *mai*

17. *octobre*

18. *janvier*

19. *mars*

16. Memorial Day occurs toward the
    end of this month: _____

17. Halloween is on the last day of
    this month: _____

18. New Year's Day is the first day of
    this month: _____

19. The month of St. Patrick's day: _____

```
S E P T E M B R E A E R U Y U
W A X G G I W I J D V R F T H
U T N B X A M Q U Z I D A K J
O E S S A M E D I B E D S C E
H L C V G G I H N I P F J L U
O L R Y H M N O V E M B R E D
J I Z M A R S M E R C R E D I
L U K N F M K A O U T R S D O
A J C L D J B R Q M C N E T C
I H Y C N A P D B D F R Q N T
E F H L U N D I K L D E X M O
Z P N Y J V T X S N P T L P B
V O I R Q I K F E V R I E R R
W A L J Y E Y V U O Z B G O E
M G C A E R W D E C E M B R E
```

Now that you have learned the names of the days and months, let's learn how to say dates. When the French want to say, "Today is Monday, July fourteenth," they say, **"C'est aujourd'hui lundi, le quatorze juillet."** "Today is Friday, March first" would be **"C'est aujourd'hui vendredi, le premier* mars."**

Your teacher will divide the class into small groups. Each of you will choose your birthday month and make up a calendar for that month. Complete the calendar with the days of the week and the month in French and enter the dates.

LUNDI						DIMANCHE

Now that you have completed your calendar, take turns pointing to several dates and saying them to your partners. Then point to the date of your birthdate and say: **Mon anniversaire est** (*My birthday is*) . . . followed by the date.

* The French use the word **premier** instead of **un** for the first day of the month. **Premier** is easy to remember because it is a cognate; when you go to a movie's *premiere*, you go to its *first* performance.

➡ Point to the classroom calendar or sketch one on the chalkboard. Point to a date and say, for example, **"C'est aujourd'hui lundi, le six octobre."** Call on students to identify other dates on the calendar.

➡ Now that students are able to say the date in French, at the beginning of each class period, have a student greet the class, say the date, and write it on the chalkboard. The student says, for example, **"Bonjour, classe. C'est aujourd'hui lundi, le six octobre."**

➡ Divide class into groups of three and have each student fill in the month, days required, and dates of the blank calendars to reflect the month of his or her birthday this year. Group members then take turns choosing different dates and telling them to one another.

➡ Model **Mon anniversaire est . . .** for students and point out that, in French, **anniversaire** may mean both *birthday* and *anniversary*.

OCTOBRE						
LUNDI	MARDI	MERCREDI	JEUDI	VENDREDI	SAMEDI	DIMANCHE
		1	2	3	4	5
6	7	8	9	10	11	12
13	14	15	16	17	18	19
20	21	22	23	24	25	26
27	28	29	30	31		

➡ Linking Dialog 2 and Section 7, "The Classroom"

Dialog 2 and Section 7 will be most effective if treated as a unit. Students need to know the names of two or three classroom objects in order to do the exercise that accompanies the dialog, and they need phrases and expressions of the dialog to discuss objects in the classroom. Students will easily learn the new words **(une fille** and **un soda)** illustrated in Dialog 2. You could choose one or two additional objects, then use the new phrases students have just learned as they practice the vocabulary in Section 7.

➡ *Claude's clues:* Model pronunciation of the French **ou** and **u** sounds for students.

➡ Before students are asked to read Dialog 2 for meaning, have them look at the characters and guess what Pierre and Solange may be saying in each illustration.

➡ Next, model pronunciation as students read the dialog.

➡ Have students close their books. Read short segments for students to repeat. If a phrase is too long, break it into shorter sections, reading the last part first.

➡ Explain that **Bonjour** means *Hello* and **Salut** means *Hi.* Wait to introduce the distinction between formal and informal greetings until the following **Activité.**

➡ Ask questions such as:

- How does Solange ask Pierre how he is?
- How does Pierre answer?
- Can you guess the difference between **Ça va bien** and **Comme ci, comme ça** by looking at the pictures?

➡ Continue asking:

- What is Pierre drawing? What is it called in French?
- What is Solange holding? What is it called in French?
- How does Pierre ask "What is this?"
- What does Solange answer?
- How does Pierre say "Thank you"?
- How does Solange say "You're welcome"?

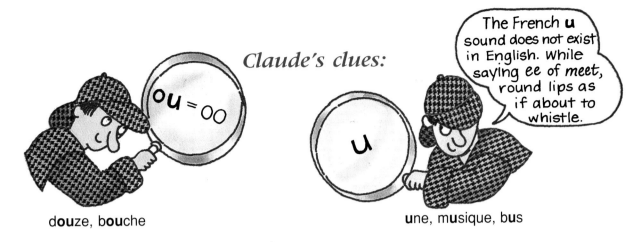

Claude's clues:

ou = OO

douze, bouche

The French **u** sound does not exist in English. While saying ee of *meet*, round lips as if about to whistle.

u

une, musique, bus

Dialog 2 *Qu'est-ce que c'est?*

ACTIVITÉ

Now let's review what you learned in Dialog 2:

1. Salut, _____ (name of friend). Ça va?

2. Comme ci, comme ça, et toi?
Ça va bien.

3. Qu'est-ce que c'est?
C'est un(e) _____.

4. Merci beaucoup.
De rien.

En France — French Holidays

What is the first thing many students look for on the school calendar? Days off. French students are given time off for the following holidays:

All Saints' Day *(la Toussaint)*: November 1. A day in celebration of the saints and a day of remembrance of relatives and friends who have passed on. The week of All Saints' Day is a week of recess for French students.

Armistice Day *(l'Armistice)*: November 11. The day that commemorates the end of World War I in 1918.

Christmas *(Noël)*: December 25. Christmas Eve is celebrated with a midnight mass and a big dinner afterward. Children put shoes under the Christmas tree. During the night, Santa Claus *(le père Noël)* puts presents into the shoes. Students enjoy two weeks vacation during Christmas and New Year.

Winter Vacation. Students have a one-week recess in February.

Good Friday *(le Vendredi Saint)* and **Easter** *(Pâques).* Sugar eggs and chocolate are given to children.

NOTE TO TEACHERS

➡ Introduce the difference between formal and informal greetings in French.

- ◆ Explain that when greeting a friend or classmate, you may say **"Salut!,"** an informal way of saying *"Hi."*
- ◆ When greeting a teacher or an adult, say **"Bonjour, monsieur (madame, mademoiselle)."**

Greet several students with **Salut!,** allowing them time to respond.

➡ Explain that **Ça va?** is an informal way of saying *"How are you?"* Students may practice **Salut!** and **Ça va?** in small groups. Have students glean as much meaning as possible from context. Refer them to the vocabulary list at the end of the book for words and phrases they do not understand.

➡ Display a pen and say, **"C'est un stylo."** Have the class repeat. Then ask, **"Qu'est-ce que c'est?"** The class answers, **"C'est un stylo."** Repeat the exercise with additional classroom items. Give students a chance to ask each other **"Qu'est-ce que c'est?"**

➡ Now is a good time to explain that French nouns, or names of objects, are either masculine or feminine and that **un** is masculine and **une** is feminine.

➡ Continue asking **"Qu'est-ce que c'est?"** while pointing to other objects in the classroom. After each question and answer, say **"Merci beaucoup."** Instruct students to respond **De rien.** Have students practice in small groups with **Qu'est-ce que c'est?, C'est un(e) _____ , Merci beaucoup,** and **De rien.**

➡ Using hand puppets, have two students improvise a skit in front of the class between two people who meet, greet, ask each other to identify several objects in the classroom, and thank each other.

ANSWERS

1. *Veteran's Day*

2. *Fourth of July, Independence Day*

3. *The first Monday of September*

En France (Supplementary Culture)

➡ Students may be interested in learning more about vacations in France. Here are some points for discussion.

The French have five weeks of paid vacation a year. Some families take a short vacation in winter and head for the mountains. Most French families take a four-week vacation in July or August. At that time, French city dwellers leave the crowded and noisy cities by the millions and head for the sun of the seacoast, the calm of the countryside, or the adventure of another country. The seacoast is the most popular vacation spot, followed by the countryside, and then the mountains. Almost a quarter of the French who take a summer vacation camp out. Paris, deserted by many of its inhabitants, becomes a haven for tourists. Many neighborhood restaurants, cafés, and shops close their doors for the entire month of August.

➡ Francophone countries celebrate their national holiday on different days: For example, in Switzerland, it's August 1; in Canada, July 1; in Algeria, July 5.

Spring Vacation. Students enjoy a two-week recess during Easter.

Labor Day *(le premier mai)*: May 1. Workers celebrate in the streets with parades. There are marches and displays organized by trade unions. The lily of the valley is considered the good-luck symbol of this day and is offered to relatives and close friends.

May 8 *(le 8 mai)* celebrates the Allied victory in 1945 and the end of World War II in Europe.

During the summer, a major national holiday, **Bastille Day** *(la Fête Nationale)*, is celebrated on July 14. This holiday marks the storming of the Bastille prison in 1789 and the beginning of the French Revolution. There are military parades, parties, dancing in the streets, and, of course, magnificent fireworks.

Assumption Day *(l'Assomption)*: August 15 is a very important summer holiday. In many towns there are religious processions and folklore festivals.

1. What is the name of the holiday on November 11 in the United States? _____

2. Which American holiday would you compare to **Bastille Day**?

_____

3. When do we celebrate Labor Day in the United States?

_____

7 The Classroom

Claude's clue:

$$\left.\begin{array}{l} o \\ au \\ eau \end{array}\right\} = oh$$

rose, stylo   Claude, aujourd'hui   beau, bureau

Learn the names of the objects in your classroom.
See how many names you can remember at a time
without having to look at the book:

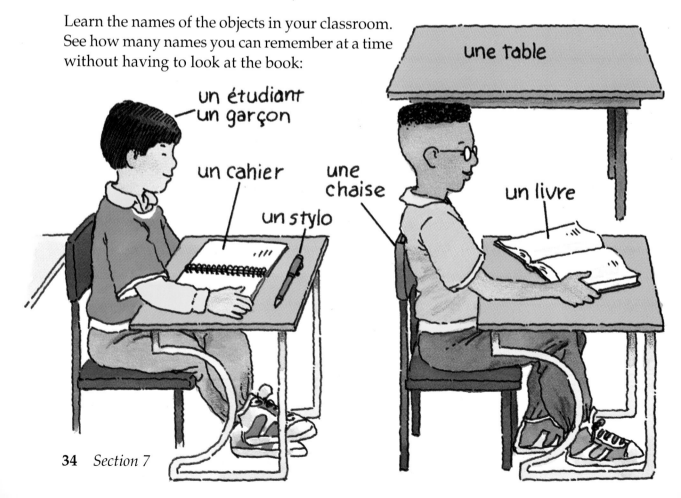

une table

un étudiant
un garçon

un cahier

une chaise

un stylo

un livre

NOTE TO TEACHERS

➡ *Claude's clues:* Model pronunciation of the French **o, au,** and **eau** sounds for students.

➡ Model pronunciation of classroom words for students.

- ◆ Point to a desk and say, **"C'est un pupitre."** Have the class repeat.
- ◆ Indicate a piece of chalk: **"C'est un morceau de craie."**
- ◆ Silently point to the first object, allowing students time to recall and repeat its name.
- ◆ Name a third object, then have class recall previous objects named.
- ◆ Continue adding items and repeating previously mentioned ones, stretching students' memories.

➡ Use picture dictation for additional reinforcement. Have students draw the object they hear.

➡ A bingo game can easily be adapted as a listening comprehension activity for classroom objects. Draw ten objects on the chalkboard. Name the objects or have students name them. Ask students to pick five of the ten objects and draw them on a piece of paper. You then name the objects at random as students check if the objects are among those on their papers. The first student to cross out all five objects is the winner.

This simple song may be adapted to practice classroom objects and adjectives. You may wish to replace these adjectives with adjectives taught later on page 50. As they sing the song, have students either point to the object in the book or mime the object with their hands and body.

Dans la Salle de Classe

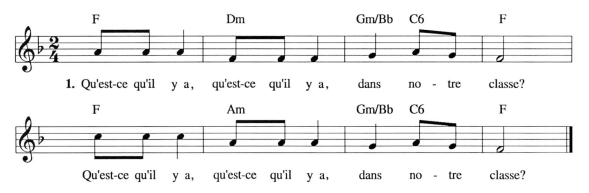

1. Qu'est-ce qu'il y a, qu'est-ce qu'il y a, dans no-tre classe?

Qu'est-ce qu'il y a, qu'est-ce qu'il y a, dans no-tre classe?

2. Un gar-çon, un gar-çon, un beau garçon.
3. U-ne fille, u-ne fille, une bel-le fille.
4. Un bu-reau, un bu-reau, un grand bu-reau.

5. Un sty-lo, un sty-lo, un sty-lo bleu.
6. Un ta-bleau, un ta-bleau, un ta-bleau noir.

Translation

IN THE CLASSROOM

1. What's in, what's in, in our classroom?
2. A boy, a boy, a cute boy.
3. A girl, a girl, a pretty girl.
4. A desk, a desk, a big desk.
5. A pen, a pen, a blue pen.
6. A chalkboard, a chalkboard, a black chalkboard.
And so on.

un tableau noir

un morceau de craie

une porte

une fenêtre

un professeur

une feuille de papier

une étudiante
une fille

un pupitre

un crayon

un bureau

In French, every noun is considered masculine or feminine. The masculine indefinite article *(a, an)* is **un**, and the feminine is **une**.

1. Name aloud as many of the classroom words in French as you can remember. Study the words you did not remember.

2. Write the name of the illustrations in French in the first column of blank lines.

3. Correct your work. Give yourself one point for each correct answer.

4. Now cover the illustrations and write the English meanings of the French words in the second column of blank lines.

5. Correct your work. Give yourself one point for each correct answer.

WRITE FRENCH WORDS HERE   WRITE ENGLISH WORDS HERE

1. _____   _____

2. _____   _____

3. _____   _____

4. _____   _____

5. _____   _____

6. _____   _____

NOTE TO TEACHERS

This activity may be done in class or at home. If done in class, allow time for students to correct their work.

ANSWERS TO ACTIVITÉ

1. *un livre*   *a book*
2. *un crayon*   *a pencil*
3. *un stylo*   *a pen*
4. *un cahier*   *a notebook*
5. *une chaise*   *a chair*
6. *une table*   *a table*

ANSWERS TO ACTIVITÉ *(continued)*

7. *un tableau noir*   *a chalkboard*

8. *un morceau de craie*   *a piece of chalk*

9. *une porte*   *a door*

10. *une fenêtre*   *a window*

11. *une feuille de papier*   *a sheet of paper*

12. *un étudiant / un garçon*   *a student /a boy*

13. *une étudiante / une fille*   *a student / a girl*

14. *un bureau*   *a teacher's desk*

15. *un pupitre*   *a student's desk*

16. *un professeur*   *a teacher*

7. _____   _____

8. _____   _____

9. _____   _____

10. _____   _____

11. _____   _____

12. _____   _____

13. _____   _____

14. _____   _____

15. _____   _____

16. _____   _____

Thirty-two points is a perfect score. If you made a mistake, you can improve your score by repeating the exercise on a blank piece of paper and correcting it again.

Classroom Vocabulary Puzzle: To solve this puzzle, first express the following words in French then fit them in the puzzle vertically and horizontally:

5-letter words

chalk __ __ __ __ __

girl __ __ __ __ __

door __ __ __ __ __

book __ __ __ __ __

pen __ __ __ __ __

table __ __ __ __ __

6-letter words

chair __ __ __ __ __ __

teacher's desk __ __ __ __ __ __

notebook __ __ __ __ __ __

paper __ __ __ __ __ __

pencil __ __ __ __ __ __

boy __ __ __ __ __ __

7-letter words

window __ __ __ __ __ __ __

student's desk __ __ __ __ __ __ __

10-letter word

teacher __ __ __ __ __ __ __ __ __ __

11-letter word combination

chalkboard __ __ __ __ __ __ __ __ __ __ __

ANSWERS TO ACTIVITÉ

5-letter words

chalk	**CRAIE**
girl	**FILLE**
door	**PORTE**
book	**LIVRE**
pen	**STYLO**
table	**TABLE**

6-letter words

chair	**CHAISE**
teacher'sdesk	**BUREAU**
notebook	**CAHIER**
paper	**PAPIER**
pencil	**CRAYON**
boy	**GARÇON**

7-letter words

window	**FENÊTRE**
student'sdesk	**PUPITRE**

10-letter word

teacher	**PROFESSEUR**

11-letter word combination

chalkboard	**TABLEAU NOIR**

ANSWERS TO ACTIVITÉ

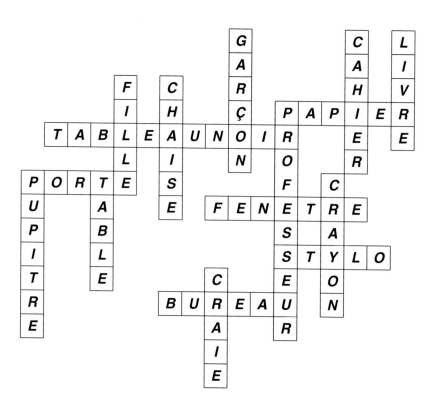

En France

School and Leisure Time

PROGRAMME
Mai
et
Juin

Guitare classique : mardi : 19h-20h
Guitare folk : jeudi 17h -18h
Poterie : vendredi 17h -18h 30 (7 à 10 ans)
   mercredi 17h -19h (11 à 14 ans)
Peinture à l'huile : mercredi 18h - 20h
Danse moderne : lundi 17h -18h
Judo : mardi 18h -19h
Atelier Théâtre : vendredi 17h-18h30
Ordinateur : jeudi 17h-18h (7 à 12 ans)
   mardi 17h-19h (13 à 16 ans)

French school children have long school days and are also required to do at least one and a half to two hours of homework a day.

French family life is also very important, and parents tend to be strict.

Because French schools normally do not sponsor activities like sports, dances, games, most students go to youth centers in their neighborhoods. Here young people gather to attend classes in music, dance, drama, arts and crafts, photography, judo, computer science, fencing, soccer, and other hobbies. Movies, plays, and weekend excursions are among the activities organized by the youth center.

1. Which sports, leisure activities, or classes are you involved in this year?

_____

2. Where do you go for these activities? _____

_____

3. Do you participate in group excursions? If yes, where did you go this year?

_____

Answers may vary.

En France (Supplementary Culture)

➡ French cities have youth centers called **Maisons des Jeunes et de la Culture.** Young people pay minimal dues and are issued I.D. cards.

➡ Although schools do not generally sponsor sports, some schools provide trips that combine schoolwork with sports and the outdoors. For example, in the winter, some middle schools sponsor, at very affordable prices, special **classes de neige** *(snow classes).* Students and teachers go off to a winter ski resort in the Alps for two to three weeks. In the morning students attend their regular school courses, and in the afternoon they learn to ski. There are also **classes de mer** on the seaside and **classes vertes** or **classes de nature** in the countryside in the fall or spring.

➡ French youngsters do many of the same things during their free time as their American counterparts. They watch television and movies, listen to music, and play video games. French youngsters spend much time with friends at one another's homes and often stay overnight on weekends. Young people in France prefer going out in groups, and it is not unusual for as many as ten to twelve young people to go places together or plan get-togethers called **boums.** A **boum** is an informal gathering, usually held on Saturday afternoons, with music, dancing, and food. Dating in France does not start until much later, usually when teenagers are sixteen or seventeen years old and more inclined to make a commitment. Going out with just one person, rather than in a group, is seen as the beginning of a more serious relationship.

➡ In the past few years, France has witnessed the construction of several large amusement parks, popular with the young and old alike. The first, built in 1987, is devoted to French fables and legends. Another offers a reconstruction of a Gaulois village as well as the reconstruction of several streets of Paris at different periods in history. In 1993, France got its own Disneyland in the outskirts of Paris. Several other amusement parks based on different themes are presently under construction.

➡ French youngsters also enjoy reading. They love to follow the antics of the young boy Nicolas and his family in the many adventures of *Le Petit Nicolas.* Also very popular are the comic books *Tintin, Asterix,* and *Spirou.*

NOTE TO TEACHERS

➡ *Claude's clue:* Model pronunciation of the French **oi** sound for students.

➡ Model pronunciation of color words. To teach colors, use crayons, paints, balloons, construction paper, and so on.

➡ You may wish to use picture dictation as a listening comprehension activity. Have students draw and color the classroom objects they hear. For example, **une table rouge, un crayon vert**.

➡ Here is a song students will enjoy to practice colors:

À Paris

1. À Pa - ris, à Pa - ris, sur un pe - tit che - val gris. À Pa - ris, à Pa - ris, sur un pe - tit che - val gris. Au pas, au pas.

2. À Rouen, à Rouen, sur un petit cheval blanc.	Au pas, au pas.
3. À Verdun, à Verdun, sur un petit cheval brun.	Au pas, au pas.
4. À la foire, à la foire, sur un petit cheval noir.	Au pas, au pas.
5. À Toulouse, à Toulouse, sur un petit cheval rouge.	Au pas, au pas.
6. À Bayeux, à Bayeux, sur un petit cheval bleu.	Au pas, au pas.
7. À Quimper, à Quimper, sur un petit cheval vert.	Au pas, au pas.
8. À Narbonne, à Narbonne, sur un petit cheval jaune.	Au pas, au pas.

Translation

IN PARIS
1. *In Paris, in Paris, on a little gray horse. Slowly, slowly.*
2. *In Rouen, in Rouen, on a little white horse.*
3. *In Verdun, in Verdun, on a little brown horse.*
4. *At the fair, at the fair, on a little black horse.*
5. *In Toulouse, in Toulouse, on a little red horse.*
6. *Bayeux – blue*
7. *Quimper – green*
8. *Narbonne – yellow*

8 *Colors*

Claude's clue:

oi = wa

n**oi**r, tr**oi**s, madem**oi**selle

jaune

orange

vert

rouge

noir

bleu

brun

rose

blanc   violet

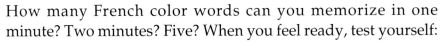

How many French color words can you memorize in one minute? Two minutes? Five? When you feel ready, test yourself:

1. Say as many French color words as you can remember.
2. Write the French color words in the first column of blank lines.
3. Check your work and give yourself one point for each correct answer.
4. Now cover the colors and write the English meanings of the French color words in the second column of blank lines.
5. Check your work and give yourself one point for each correct answer.

WRITE FRENCH WORDS HERE	WRITE ENGLISH WORDS HERE
1. _____	_____
2. _____	_____
3. _____	_____
4. _____	_____
5. _____	_____
6. _____	_____
7. _____	_____
8. _____	_____
9. _____	_____
10. _____	_____

Did you get 20 points? If not, try again with a blank piece of paper.

NOTE TO TEACHERS

The **Activité** may be done in class or as homework.

ANSWERS TO ACTIVITÉ

1. *rouge*   **red**
2. *orange*   **orange**
3. *jaune*   **yellow**
4. *vert*   **green**
5. *bleu*   **blue**
6. *violet*   **purple**
7. *rose*   **pink**
8. *blanc*   **white**
9. *brun*   **brown**
10. *noir*   **black**

NOTE TO TEACHERS

Students will receive instructions in how to form feminine adjectives in Section 10, "Talking About Yourself." For now, if students want to describe feminine objects, remind them of **enchanté(e)** with its additional **e** and have them memorize **violette** and **blanche.**

Here are pictures of items you have already learned.

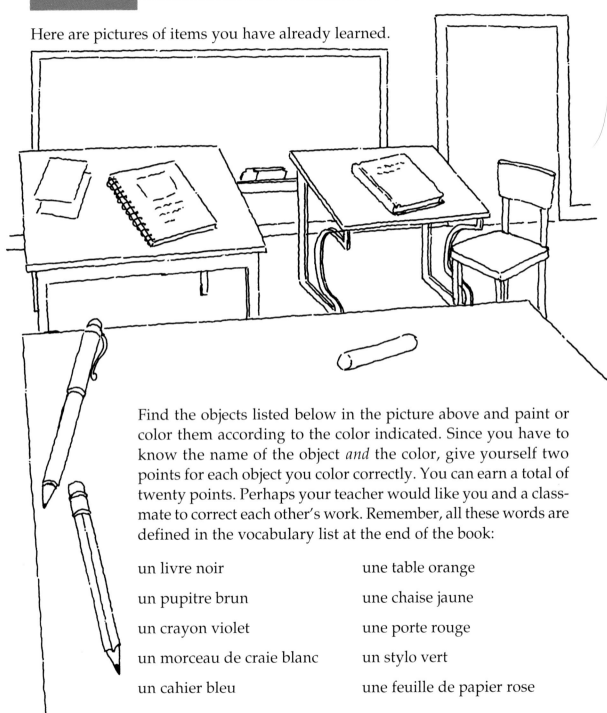

Find the objects listed below in the picture above and paint or color them according to the color indicated. Since you have to know the name of the object *and* the color, give yourself two points for each object you color correctly. You can earn a total of twenty points. Perhaps your teacher would like you and a classmate to correct each other's work. Remember, all these words are defined in the vocabulary list at the end of the book:

un livre noir

un pupitre brun

un crayon violet

un morceau de craie blanc

un cahier bleu

une table orange

une chaise jaune

une porte rouge

un stylo vert

une feuille de papier rose

You've already seen this map of the world. Color all the countries where French is spoken. Color the countries in each continent according to the colors below:

Europe — **jaune**   South America — **rouge**

Africa — **bleu**   North America — **vert**

Island Countries — **orange**

NOTE TO TEACHERS

➡ Have students also name the countries where French is spoken.

➡ As a research project, you may wish students to find the colors of the flags of French-speaking countries. Assign different areas or continents to individual students or groups of students. Students draw, color, and name the colors of the flags. As a class activity, have students collaborate on a color poster of a map and/or the flags of the French-speaking countries.

➡ Here are the colors of the flags of the countries that appear on the map on pages 4 and 5.

Belgium: black/yellow/red
Corsica: French flag
France: blue/white/red
Luxembourg: red/white/blue
Monaco: red/white
Switzerland: red with white cross

Guadeloupe: French flag
Haiti: blue/red with palm tree emblem
Martinique: French flag

New Caledonia: French flag
Tahiti: French flag

Canada: red/white/red with red maple leaf
Saint Pierre and Miquelon: French flag
Quebec: white/blue with white fleurs-de-lis
Louisiana and New England: American flag

French Guiana: French flag

Cambodia: red/blue with yellow emblem
Vietnam: red with yellow star
Algeria: green/white with red moon and star

Benin: green/yellow/red
Burkina Faso: red/green with yellow star
Burundi: red/white/green with three green and red stars
Cameroon: green/red/yellow with yellow star
Central African Republic: blue/white/green/yellow/red with yellow star
Chad: blue/yellow/red
Congo: green/orange/red
Djibouti: blue/green/white with red star
Gabon: green/yellow/blue
Guinea: red/yellow/green
Ivory Coast: orange/white/green
Madagascar: white/red/green
Mali: green/yellow/red
Mauritania: green with yellow moon and star
Morocco: red with green star
Niger: orange/green/white with red circle
Rwanda: red/yellow/green with black R
Senegal: green/yellow/red with green star
Togo: green/yellow/red with white star
Tunisia: red/white circle with red moon and star
Zaire: green/yellow circle with black arm holding torch

NOTE TO TEACHERS

➡ *Claude's clue:* Model pronunciation of words ending with silent consonants. For additional practice, have students find words ending with silent consonant in vocabulary already learned: numbers, page 16; days of the week, page 22; months of the year, page 24; classroom objects, page 34; and colors, page 41.

➡ At this point, have students learn definite articles. Having previously learned **un** and **une** and the concept of gender, the addition of **le, la,** and **l'** follows logically. Explain that **l'œil** is masculine and **l'oreille** is feminine.

➡ Some students may ask how to tell the gender of a French noun. Since there are no simple formulas, you may wish to suggest that students memorize the article along with each noun they learn.

➡ Use picture dictation for additional reinforcement. Have students draw the part of the body they hear.

➡ A bingo game can easily be adapted as a listening comprehension activity for parts of the body vocabulary. Follow the instructions for a similar activity on page 34.

9 *The Body*

Claude's clue:

Final consonants are often not pronounced.

nez, pied, bras

la tête
l'œil
le nez
la bouche
la main
l'oreille
le bras
la jambe
le pied

When you want to talk about yourself in French, you will need to know the names of the parts of the body. How many names can you remember without having to look at the book?

You have already learned that the masculine article **un** and the feminine article **une** mean *a, an*. Now let's learn how to express English *the*. Did you notice the words **le**, **la**, and **l'** before all of the nouns? To say *the*, French uses three words: **le** before masculine nouns that start with a consonant; **la** before feminine nouns that start with a consonant; and **l'** before masculine or feminine nouns that start with a vowel or with **h**.

Fill in the names of the parts of the body:

Choose a partner. Point to each other's hand, foot, and so on, and ask, **"Qu'est-ce que c'est?"** Answer, **"C'est une main." "C'est un pied."** And so on.

ANSWERS TO ACTIVITÉ

head	**la tête**	eye	**l'œil**
ear	**l'oreille**	nose	**le nez**
mouth	**la bouche**	hand	**la main**
arm	**le bras**	foot	**le pied**
leg	**la jambe**		

NOTE TO TEACHERS

➡ Model the second **Activité** with a student in front of the class.

➡ Here is a song students will enjoy to practice parts of the body words. As the class sings the song, have students make gestures to accompany the words: planting with the hands, moving the part of the body mentioned, or pointing to it.

Savez-vous Planter les Choux?

1. Sa - vez - vous plan - ter les choux À la mo - de, à la
mo - de Sa - vez - vous plan - ter les choux À la mo - de de chez nous?

2. On les plante avec le pied,
À la mode, à la mode
On les plante avec le pied,
À la mode de chez nous.

3. On les plante avec la main,
À la mode, à la mode
On les plante avec la main,
À la mode de chez nous.

4. . . . avec le bras . . .
5. . . . avec le nez . . .
6. . . . avec la jambe . . .
7. . . . avec l'oreille . . .
8. . . . avec la bouche . . .

Translation   DO YOU KNOW HOW TO PLANT CABBAGES?

1. Do you know how to plant cabbages
In the way, in the way
Do you know how to plant cabbages
In the way, in the way we do at home?
2. We plant them with the hand,
In the way, in the way
We plant them with the hand,
In the way, in the way we do at home.

3. We plant them with the foot,
In the way, in the way
We plant them with the foot,
In the way, in the way we do at home.
4. . . . with the nose . . .
5. . . . with the arm . . .
6. . . . with the leg . . .
7. . . . with the ear . . .

ANSWERS TO ACTIVITÉ

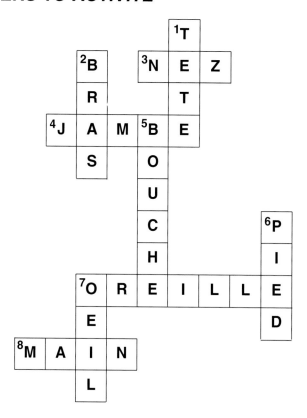

Simon dit: One row of students plays at a time while the rest of the class watches to see who makes a mistake and is eliminated. Have students take turns leading each row. If the leader says, **"Simon dit: la bouche,"** students should point to their mouth or make it move. If the leader simply says, **"la bouche,"** students should remain still. When all rows have played, the winner of each row plays the final round in front of the class.

Complete this crossword puzzle with the
French names of the parts of the body:

Across

3.

4.

7.

8.

Down

1.

2.

5.

6.

7.

"Simon dit" means *"Simon says."* Move or point to that part of
the body Simon refers to only if you hear the words **"Simon dit."**
If you do not hear the words **"Simon dit,"** don't move at all.

En France · Gestures

In every culture, gestures play an important role in communicating ideas and feelings. Gestures may be accompanied by a word or phrase. In most situations, however, the meaning of a gesture is clear to a native speaker or listener. Gestures, like pictures, are often more expressive than words and contribute to a more lively conversation.

Here are some typical French gestures:

1. One, two, three . . .

[The French start counting with their thumb.]

2. Hi!

[The French kiss on both cheeks to greet relatives and friends. In some parts of France, three kisses and even four are exchanged.]

3. Wonderful!

4. You must be kidding!

En France (Supplementary Culture)

➡ Students may enjoy these additional notes on gestures:

- ◆ The French shake hands when they meet and take leave. Unlike the American handshake, which consists of gripping the hand and raising and lowering it several times, the French handshake consists of a single firm grip. French males shake hands much more frequently than their American counterparts.

- ◆ Female friends exchange kisses on the cheek. So do males and their female friends. Men may sometimes embrace each other, but they don't kiss. Kissing on the lips is reserved for lovers.

- ◆ Another common French facial gesture is used when saying the word "bof," roughly *uhhh* in English. It involves puffing out the cheeks with a slight, plosive emission of air and expresses pondering, resignation, or mild disgust.

Sample Answers to Activité

1. Waving the hand for good-bye. Holding one's stomach with the hand for "I'm hungry."

   To and fro of second finger for "No, no."

   Shaking the head no.

   Nodding the head yes.

   Shrugging the shoulders for "I don't know."

   Arms folded and foot tapping to show impatience.

   Thumbs up for "A-OK."

2. Answers will vary.

5. I've had it up to here.

6. Not a penny. Nothing!

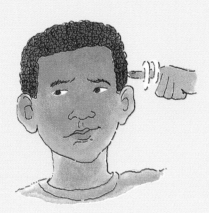

7. You must be crazy!

8. I don't know.

1. Can you think of gestures Americans use to express their feelings or ideas?

_____

_____

2. What gestures do you use? _____

_____

_____

10 Talking About Yourself

Claude's clue:

When a word ends in **e**, the consonant before the **e** is pronounced.

for~~t~~ forte   lai~~d~~ lai**d**e   gro~~s~~ gro**ss**e

An adjective describes a person or thing. In the sentence "The beautiful girl is happy," *beautiful* and *happy* are adjectives that describe *girl*. Many adjectives are easy to remember if you think of them in pairs:

mince   gros   intelligent   stupide

triste   content   petit   grand

beau   laid   fort   faible

NOTE TO TEACHERS

➡ *Claude's clue:* Model pronunciation of words ending in **e** preceded by a pronounced consonant. For additional practice, have students find similar words in vocabulary already learned: numbers, page 16; days of the week, page 22; months of the year, page 26; the classroom, page 34 and 35; and colors, page 41.

➡ Model pronunciation of adjectives. To teach adjectives, have a student mime adjectives while the class tries to guess the adjective being acted out.

➡ Have students find cognates among the adjectives. Point out any they miss: **intelligent, stupide, grand, content.** Explain that **content** and **grand** have somewhat different meanings in French.

➡ Point out that **beau** is *beautiful.* Explain that **beau** and **belle** are also English cognates and ask students whether they have heard of *beau* meaning boyfriend and *belle* referring to a beautiful young woman, as in Southern belle or the belle of the ball.

ANSWERS TO ACTIVITÉ

1. *triste*   2. *content*   3. *intelligent*

4. *stupide*   5. *mince*   6. *gros*

7. *petit*   8. *grand*   9. *fort*

10. *faible*   11. *beau*   12. *laid*

NOTE TO TEACHERS

➡ When students have completed the **Activité**, you may ask them to name as well as describe the objects illustrated. Note: All illustrated objects are masculine in gender.

◆ **Le livre mince.**	**Le livre gros.**
◆ **Le tableau noir intelligent.**	**Le tableau noir stupide.**
◆ **Le cahier triste.**	**Le cahier content.**
◆ **Le bureau fort.**	**Le bureau faible.**

➡ You may wish students to use **est** (*is*) and describe the objects using complete sentences.

- ◆ **Le livre est gros.**
- ◆ **Le stylo est beau.**
- ◆ **Le crayon est petit.**
- ◆ **Le cahier est content.** And so on.

Cover page 50 with a sheet of paper and write the French adjectives that describe the objects you see:

1. _____   2. _____   3. _____

4. _____   5. _____   6. _____

7. _____   8. _____   9. _____

10. _____   11. _____   12. _____

NOTE TO TEACHERS

➡ Before students are asked to read Dialog 3 for meaning, have them guess what Pierre and Solange may be feeling and saying in each illustration.

➡ Next, model pronunciation either by reading aloud or by playing the cassette while students read the dialog.

➡ Now, have students read the dialog for meaning. Have them glean as much meaning as possible from context. Refer them to the vocabulary list at the end of the book for words and phrases they do not understand.

➡ Explain that **je suis** means *I am,* and **tu es** means *you are.* Point out that **pourquoi** means *why* and **parce que** means *because.*

NOTE TO TEACHERS *(Optional Dialog 4, page 53)*

➡ Dialog 4 is provided for teachers who wish to introduce **Vous** and other formal expressions. You may reproduce it for your students. Dialog 4 may be presented at the end of Section 10, "Talking About Yourself."

➡ Before students are asked to read Dialog 4 for meaning, have them scan the dialog for familiar words and expressions and guess the general content of the conversation.

➡ Model pronunciation either by reading aloud or by playing cassette while students read dialog.

➡ Have students close their books. Read short segments for students to repeat.

➡ Ask questions:
   ◆ How do Solange and Pierre greet each other in the evening?
   ◆ How does Solange àsk Pierre, "Who is that?"
   ◆ What is the woman's profession?
   ◆ How does Solange ask the woman her name?
   ◆ How does the French teacher ask Solange her name?
   ◆ How do the French say, "His name is ____"?
   ◆ How does Pierre ask the French teacher how she is?

➡ Point out difference between formal and informal expressions:

Comment vous appelez-vous?	**Comment t'appelles-tu?**
Vous êtes . . .	**Tu es . . .**
Comment allez-vous?	**Ça va?**

➡ New vocabulary and expressions:

Bonsoir.	*Good evening.*
Qui est-ce?	*Who is that?*
C'est le professeur de français.	*That's the French teacher.*
Comment vous appelez-vous?	*What's your name? (formal)*
Comment s'appelle-t-elle?	*What's her name?*
Je ne sais pas.	*I don't know.*
Il (Elle) s'appelle . . .	*His (Her) name is . . .*
Vous êtes le professeur de français.	*You are the French teacher. (formal)*
N'est-ce pas?	*Right? Isn't that so?*
Comment allez-vous?	*How are you? (formal)*

Dialog 4 *(Optional)*

Bonsoir

Solange and Pierre meet at an international school fair organized by the foreign language department of their school. It is 7 P.M.

Solange:	**Bonsoir, Pierre.**
Pierre:	**Bonsoir, Solange.**

Solange points to a woman.

Solange:	**Qui est-ce?**
Pierre:	**C'est le professeur de français.**
Solange:	**Comment s'appelle-t-elle?**
Pierre:	**Je ne sais pas.**

Solange walks toward the French teacher.

Solange:	**Bonsoir, Madame. Vous êtes le professeur de français, n'est-ce pas?**
Mme Daudet:	**Oui. Comment t'appelles-tu?**
Solange:	**Je m'appelle Solange Artaud. Et vous, comment vous appelez-vous?**
Mme Daudet:	**Je m'appelle Sylvie Daudet.**

Solange and Madame Daudet shake hands.

Solange:	**Enchantée, Madame.**
Mme Daudet:	**Enchantée, Solange.**

Solange gestures to Pierre to join them.

Solange:	**Il s'appelle Pierre.**
Mme Daudet:	**Bonsoir, Pierre. Je m'appelle Sylvie Daudet.**
Pierre:	**Enchanté, Madame Daudet. Comment allez-vous?**
Mme Daudet:	**Très bien, merci.**

Let's take a closer look at some of the words you learned in Dialog 3:

Je suis . . .

Tu es . . .

Il est . . .
Le garçon est . . .

Elle est . . .
La fille est . . .

➡ Have class repeat, **"Je suis triste."** Then say, **"mince."** The class repeats, **"Je suis mince."**

➡ Continue with **faible. (Triste, mince, faible,** and **stupide** are pronounced the same way in masculine and feminine forms. Limit yourself to these adjectives until after the next section.)

➡ Follow the same procedure with **tu es.**

➡ Present **le garçon est/la fille est** and **il est/elle est.**

Practice these three forms of **être** until the class has mastered them.

➡ You may wish to practice these forms with photographs, magazine pictures, cartoons, and so on. Have students describe the people in the pictures.

NOTE TO TEACHERS

➡ You may wish to remind students that they have already learned to form the feminine of the adjective **enchanté** by adding **e.**

➡ You may wish to use picture dictation as a listening comprehension activity. Have students first write and then draw what they hear, for example: **La fille est contente. Le garçon est grand.** Have students check and correct each other's pictures and phrases. You may wish to create a composite poster of student drawings and written descriptions for display in the classroom.

Look at the adjectives on the left that could describe a boy. Compare them with the adjectives on the right that could describe a girl:

content	contente
fort	forte
grand	grande
intelligent	intelligente
laid	laide
petit	petite

French adjectives, like French nouns, have a gender. A feminine adjective is used to describe a feminine noun and a masculine adjective is used to describe a masculine noun. Which letter do we add to the masculine adjective to get the feminine?

ACTIVITÉ

Use as many adjectives on page 55 as possible to describe these animals:

_____   _____

_____   _____

_____   _____

ACTIVITÉ

Now let's learn more about adjectives. After reading the explanations, fill in the blanks with the correct form of the adjective that describes the people and animals in the pictures:

Enchantée, Richard.

Enchanté, Hélène.

1. You have already learned that when a word ends in **é**, like **enchanté**, adding an **e** creates the feminine form:

Le garçon est _____.

La fille est _____.

ANSWERS TO FIRST ACTIVITÉ

grand	*petite*
laid	*intelligente*
fort	*forte*
content	*contente*

 ## NOTE TO TEACHERS

➡ For the second **Activité,** model pronunciation for students, repeating and filling in missing words.

ANSWERS TO SECOND ACTIVITÉ

1. Le garçon est **enchanté**.
   La fille est **enchantée**.

ANSWERS *(continued)*

2. La fille est ***triste***.
Le professeur est ***triste*** aussi.

Le garçon est ***faible***.
La fille est ***faible*** aussi.

3. Il est ***gros***.
Elle est ***grosse***.

4. Le chat est ***beau***.
La chatte est ***belle***.

 # NOTE TO TEACHERS

➡ For additional practice, have students find and describe magazine pictures of movie and television stars, athletes, cartoon characters, and so on. Students may also enjoy bringing in photographs of family members or friends. Have students describe the people in their pictures to their classmates, for example:

Goofy est stupide. / Il est stupide.
Michael Jordan est grand. / Il est grand.
Roseanne Arnold est grosse. / Elle est grosse.

You may also wish students to name the people in their pictures before describing them:

Il s'appelle Superman. Superman est fort.
Elle s'appelle Sylvie. Elle est belle.

2. Mince, stupide, triste, and **faible** do not change in the feminine because they already end in **e**:

La fille est ——————————————.

Le professeur est ———————————— aussi.

Le garçon est ——————————————.

La fille est ———————————— aussi.

3. Gros becomes **grosse:**

Il est ——————————————.

Elle est ——————————————.

4. Beau becomes **belle:**

Le chat est ——————————————.

La chatte est ——————————————.

ACTIVITÉ

1. How many of the boys in this basketball team can you describe? Write the adjective that best describes each player next to his number in the column of blank lines:

GARÇONS

1	_____
2	_____
3	_____
4	_____
5	_____
6	_____
7	_____
8	_____
9	_____
10	_____

ANSWERS TO ACTIVITÉ

GARÇONS

1	*beau*
2	*content*
3	*grand*
4	*faible*
5	*gros*
6	*fort*
7	*triste*
8	*mince*
9	*petit*
10	*intelligent*

ANSWERS TO ACTIVITÉ

FILLES

1	*grosse*
2	*contente*
3	*intelligente*
4	*triste*
5	*petite*
6	*mince*
7	*forte*
8	*grande*
9	*faible*
10	*belle*

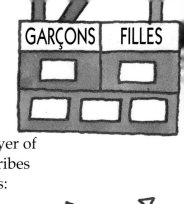

2. How would you change the adjectives to describe each player of the opposing girls' team? Write the adjective that best describes each player next to her number in the column of blank lines:

FILLES

1 _____
2 _____
3 _____
4 _____
5 _____
6 _____
7 _____
8 _____
9 _____
10 _____

ACTIVITÉ

Your teacher will now divide you into small groups to practice describing yourself and one another.

ACTIVITÉ

Play charades with the adjectives you have learned. Your teacher will divide the class into teams, and a member from one team will stand in front of the class and act out the various ways he or she would look if sad, intelligent, fat, and so on.

NOTE TO TEACHERS

➡ Have students practice describing one another in groups of three or four. Demonstrate with two or three students in front of the class.

Je suis fort(e)! Tu es fort(e) aussi.

Non, je suis faible. Mais je suis intelligent(e).

Tu es triste?

Non, je suis content(e). Et je suis très beau (belle)!

➡ You may wish to use this writing activity to reinforce and review structures and vocabulary learned in this section:

- Make a copy of the dialog on pages 52 and 53 and white-out the text in the bubbles.

- Divide the students into pairs and distribute a dialog to each student.

- Have partners create a dialog to be inserted in the empty bubbles. Refer students to the vocabulary list at the end of the book for words and phrases they need.

- Circulate among students, advising, correcting, and answering questions.

- When dialogs have been completed and corrected, have students memorize and dramatize them for the class.

Answers will vary.

En France (Supplementary Culture)

➡ Additional cultural notes on sports.

- The entire July 1989 issue of *National Geographic* is devoted to France and is an excellent source for many cultural topics. Of particular interest are the photographs of the Tour de France.

- Although the French take great interest in winning soccer teams, they spend less time watching sports and more time playing than Americans tend to do.

- Soccer is the national sport in France. Basketball as well as rugby and volleyball are growing in popularity.

- The French refer to soccer as **le football.** Football is referred to as **le football américain.**

- Tennis is also a very popular sport, and French tennis players like Henri Leconte and Yanik Noah have reached international acclaim.

- The picturesque and extensive mountain ranges of France make downhill as well as cross-country skiing an accessible and popular winter sport. During winter vacation, many French families and school-organized groups of children as young as ten years of age enjoy a skiing vacation in the Alps.

- Windsurfing and kayaking have recently become popular, especially with the young.

- Bicycling and soccer are also popular in many francophone countries, especially in Belgium and Algeria. In Quebec, ice hockey is a favorite sport, and in Switzerland, mountain climbing, skiing, and target shooting are popular.

En France Sports

In France, soccer (**le football**) is the national sport. All of the larger French cities have home teams. Each team can be identified by the distinctive colors of its uniform. The best soccer teams compete for the national championship, and there are also international matches between the best professional soccer teams in Europe and in the world. On Sunday afternoons, amateurs play on soccer teams organized by groups of friends, clubs, companies, and municipalities.

Le Tour de France, which takes place annually in June and July, is the longest and best-known bicycle race in the world. 130 to 200 participants from many countries compete in this spectacular event, which lasts over a twenty-day period and covers more than 1,500 miles. Each year, a different French city is chosen as the starting point, with Paris always the final destination. The winner of the race receives a large sum of money, but, more importantly, becomes a national hero in his country.

1. Which sports are most popular in America? _____

_____

2. Which sports do you like to play, and which ones do you just like to watch?

_____

_____

11 Recycling French

Your teacher will now give you time to use your French. Think of all you have learned!

- You can say your name!
- You can count and do math!
- You can name the days of the week and the months of the year!

- You can name objects in the classroom with their colors!
- You can describe yourself and others and point out parts of the body!

When someone asks if you can speak French: **Parles-tu français?**, now you can answer: **Oui, je parle français!**

ACTIVITÉ

Fill in the boxes with the French meanings and you will find a mystery word in one of the longest vertical columns. Write the mystery word in French and English in the blanks provided:

1. seven
2. Tuesday
3. October
4. window
5. blue
6. Good evening.
7. Hi!
8. Thank you.
9. red
10. ear

_____

_____

➥ As a culminating activity, give students the opportunity to make an oral presentation of a cultural topic studied. You may wish to divide the class into small groups with each student contributing to the research of the topic. The group then chooses a representative to speak in front the class.

➥ Now would be a good time to teach **Parles-tu français?** and **Je parle français.** Give students a chance both to ask and answer the question.

ANSWERS TO ACTIVITÉ

Mystery word: *professeur*
                 teacher

1.	S	E	P	T				
2.		M	A	R	D	I		
3.	O	C	T	O	B	R	E	
4.				F	E	N	E	T	R	E
5.		B	L	E	U			
6.	B	O	N	S	O	I	R	
7.				S	A	L	U	T
8.			M	E	R	C	I	
9.		R	O	U	G	E		
10.			O	R	E	I	L	L	E

ANSWERS TO ACTIVITÉ *(Colors will vary.)*

1. *la tête*

2. *la bouche*

3. *l'œil*

4. *l'oreille*

5. *le nez*

6. *la main*

7. *la jambe*

8. *le pied*

9. *le bras*

NOTE TO TEACHERS

➡ Have students correct each other's work as you circulate among the class, checking students' answers.

➡ For additional speaking practice of vocabulary and the verb **être,** you may wish to have students show their colored monster picture to the class and describe its colors in complete sentences. Students point to a part of the body and say, for example, "**Le nez est rouge.**"

Model a masculine and a feminine example before students begin:

> **Le nez est violet.**
>
> **La tête est verte.**

Have the class play the role of teacher and correct classmates' errors in French.

Colors: What would this funny monster look like if you could color the parts of its body? Write the names of the parts of the body and colors you would choose in the blanks below. Then color the parts of the body in the picture:

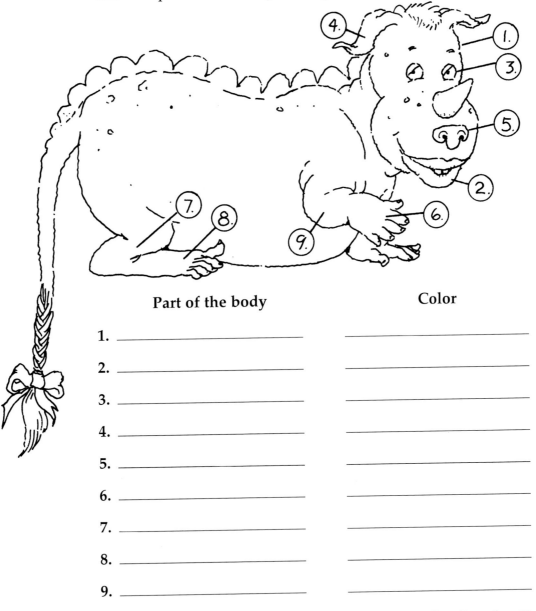

Part of the body	Color
1.	
2.	
3.	
4.	
5.	
6.	
7.	
8.	
9.	

Can you complete these dialogs or express the following ideas in French?

1. You overhear the conversation of these two people, who are meeting for the first time. Complete the dialog:

Sample Answers to Activité

1. Girl: *Bonjour, comment t'appelles-tu?*

   Boy: *Salut, je m'appelle Pierre. Et toi?*

   Girl: *Je m'appelle Solange. Enchantée.*

   Boy: *Enchanté. Ça va?*

   Girl: *Ça va très bien, et toi?*

   Boy: *Comme ci, comme ça.*

Sample Answers (continued)

1. Girl: *Au revoir, Pierre.*

    Boy: *Au revoir, Solange.*

2. Peter: *Qu'est-ce que c'est?*

    Brother: *C'est un livre.*

    Peter: *Qu'est-ce que c'est?*

    Brother: *C'est un stylo?*

2. Peter is teaching some French words to his little brother. Complete the dialog:

3. What do you think these friends are saying to each other?

4. What are the colors of the French flag?

_____ _____ _____

5. What are the names of these parts of the body?

 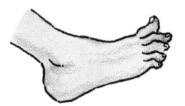 

_____ _____ _____

Sample Answers *(continued)*

3. Girl: *Merci*

   Boy: *De rien.*

4. *bleu*   *blanc*   *rouge*

5. *bouche*   *pied*   *main*

ANSWERS TO ACTIVITÉ *(continued)*

6.

janvier	
9	lundi
10	*mardi*
11	mercredi
12	*jeudi*
13	vendredi
14	*samedi*
15	*dimanche*

7. *avril*   *août*   *décembre*

8. *content*   *triste*   *forte*

6. What days of the week are missing from this agenda?

7. What month is it?

_____   _____   _____

8. What adjectives describe these young people?

_____   _____   _____

Loto is played like Bingo, except that our **Loto** game is played with words. Select French words from categories in the vocabulary list on pages 70 to 73 as directed by your teacher. Write one word across in each square at random from the chosen categories.

Your teacher will read the **Loto** words in English. If one of the French words on your card matches the English word you hear, mark that square with a small star. When you have five stars in a row, either horizontally, vertically, or diagonally, call out, **"J'ai gagné!"** (*"I won!"*)

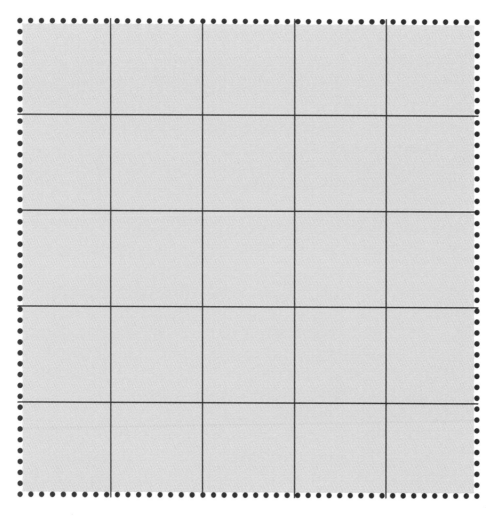

NOTE TO TEACHERS

➡ Explain that the French game **Loto** is the equivalent of Bingo.

➡ Model **J'ai gagné** *(I won)* for students.

➡ Choose categories of vocabulary you wish students to review. Complete a bingo board with 25 words from the chosen categories. Read or have students take turns reading the words aloud for the class.

➡ Check to see if a word has been spelled correctly before declaring a student a winner.

NOTE TO TEACHERS

➡ As students have encountered the French people and their language, they have probably been both amused and impressed by the differences encountered. Now is an excellent time to reinforce respect for American and French cultures alike and foster appreciation of cultural differences.

Sample Answers

➡ You may wish to discuss further how Americans generally greet one another. Ask students how they and their parents greet close family members, relatives, good friends, and acquaintances.

FRENCH	AMERICAN
2. Middle-school students have half a day of school on Wednesday and Saturday.	Middle-school students have a full-day of school on Wednesday and no school on Saturday.
3. Santa Claus puts presents into shoes that children leave under the Christmas tree.	Santa Claus puts presents into socks that are hung near the Christmas tree.
4. The national holiday is celebrated on the 14th of July.	The national holiday is celebrated on the 4th of July.
5. Schools do not sponsor sports or leisure activities. Children go to youth centers to play sports, take classes, or go on trips.	Schools sponsor sports, games, and school trips.
6. Soccer and cycling are the most popular sports.	Football, basketball, baseball, and hockey are the most popular sports.

En France

Vivent les différences! *(Hurrah for the differences!)*

Now that you have learned quite a bit about the French language and about France and its people, can you list the differences that impressed you most between French and American people? Jog your memory by looking over cultural pages 15, 23, 32–33, 40, 48–49, and 61.

An example is given to get you started:

FRENCH	AMERICAN
1. *Friends and relatives greet each other with kisses on both cheeks.*	*Friends and relatives say "Hi" and may kiss women on the cheek.*
2.	
3.	
4.	
5.	
6.	

Vocabulary

Numbers

un	1
deux	2
trois	3
quatre	4
cinq	5
six	6
sept	7
huit	8
neuf	9
dix	10
onze	11
douze	12
treize	13
quatorze	14
quinze	15
seize	16
dix-sept	17
dix-huit	18
dix-neuf	19
vingt	20
vingt et un	21
vingt-deux	22
vingt-trois	23
vingt-quatre	24
vingt-cinq	25
vingt-six	26
vingt-sept	27
vingt-huit	28
vingt-neuf	29
trente	30
trente et un	31
trente-deux	32
trente-trois	33
trente-quatre	34
trente-cinq	35
trente-six	36
trente-sept	37
trente-huit	38
trente-neuf	39
quarante	40

Arithmetic

combien?	how many?
et	plus
font	equal
moins	minus

Days of the week

lundi	Monday
mardi	Tuesday
mercredi	Wednesday
jeudi	Thursday
vendredi	Friday
samedi	Saturday
dimanche	Sunday

Months of the year

janvier	January
février	February
mars	March
avril	April
mai	May
juin	June
juillet	July
août	August
septembre	September
octobre	October
novembre	November
décembre	December

The Classroom

un bureau	a (teacher's) desk
un cahier	a notebook
une chaise	a chair
un crayon	a pencil
un étudiant	a (male) student
une étudiante	a (female) student
une fenêtre	a window
une feuille de papier	a sheet of paper
une fille	a girl
un garçon	a boy
un livre	a book
un morceau de craie	a piece of chalk
une porte	a door
un professeur	a teacher
un pupitre	a (student's) desk
un stylo	a ballpoint pen
une table	a table
un tableau noir	a chalkboard

Colors

blanc, blanche	white
bleu, bleue	blue
brun, brune	brown
jaune	yellow
noir, noire	black
orange	orange
rose	pink
rouge	red
vert, verte	green
violet, violette	purple

The Body

la bouche	the mouth
le bras	the arm
la jambe	the leg
la main	the hand
le nez	the nose
l'œil	the eye
l'oreille	the ear
le pied	the foot
la tête	the head

Adjectives

beau, belle	handsome, beautiful
content, contente	happy
enchanté, enchantée	pleased to meet you
faible	weak
fort, forte	strong
grand, grande	tall
gros, grosse	fat
intelligent, intelligente	intelligent
laid, laide	ugly
mince	thin
petit, petite	short, small
stupide	stupid
triste	sad

Expressions and phrases

Comment t'appelles-tu?	What's your name?
Je m'appelle . . .	My name is . . .
Enchanté(e).	Pleased to meet you.
Ça va?	How's it going?
Ça va bien.	Everything's fine.
Comme ci, comme ça.	So, so.
Et toi?	And you?
C'est aujourd'hui . . .	Today is . . .
Mon anniversaire est . . .	My birthday is . . .
Qu'est-ce que c'est?	What is it? / What's that?
C'est . . .	It is . . . / That is . . .
Pour toi.	For you.
Bonjour.	Hello.
Salut!	Hi!
Au revoir.	Good-bye. See you.
Je suis . . .	I am . . .
Tu es . . .	You are . . .
Il est . . .	He is . . .

Elle est . . .	She is . . .
La fille est . . .	The girl is . . .
Le garçon est . . .	The boy is . . .
Es-tu . . .?	Are you . . .?
Merci (beaucoup).	Thank you (very much).
De rien.	You're welcome.
Parles-tu français?	Do you speak French?
Je parle français.	I speak French.
J'ai gagné.	I won.
Oui.	Yes.
Non.	No.
monsieur	Mister, sir
mademoiselle	Miss
madame	madam, Mrs.
aussi	also
et	and
le chat	the (male) cat
la chatte	the (female) cat
le premier	the first
maintenant	now
pourquoi?	why?
parce que	because
un soda	carbonated fruit drink
très	very